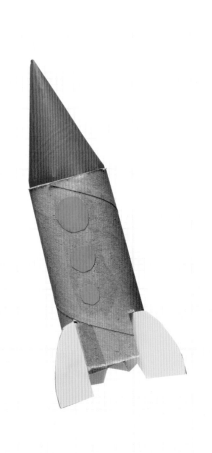

# NATIONAL GEOGRAPHIC
## KiDS

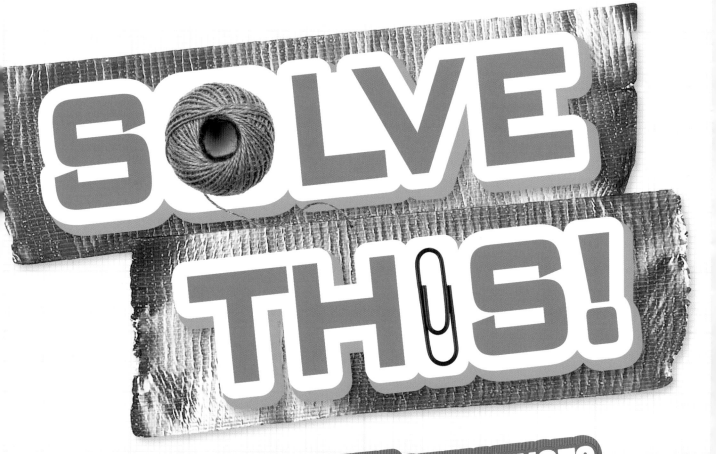

# SOLVE THIS!

## WILD AND WACKY CHALLENGES
## FOR THE GENIUS ENGINEER IN YOU

JOAN MARIE GALAT

# >> CONTENTS

## Section 3

# FOREWORD

**SUPPOSE YOU WANTED TO SOLVE A PESKY PROBLEM—AN ITCHY BACK.** Engineers design and build things—from the machine that built the book in your hand to the buildings around you. How do they figure out how to make such complex structures? By figuring out how one action leads to another, how to transfer energy, and how to get work done.

## BACK-SCRATCHING DEVICE

1. Person turns page of book
2. Turning page (cause) creates breeze, blowing feathers off scale (effect)
3. Balance tips (kinetic energy), knocking ball onto ramp
4. Ball strikes clock hand (kinetic energy), turning time to noon
5. Cuckoo action draws saw across string (potential energy)
6. Broken string (cause) drops monkey figure (effect) onto raised end of seesaw
7. Tipping seesaw hurls magnet at heavy chain, forming pendulum (potential energy)
8. Swinging chain strikes bowling pin (cause), knocking it into the next pin (effect)
9. Last bowling pin (chain reaction) knocks rock (effect) onto bicycle pedal
10. Wheel spins (kinetic energy), rotating gears (torque) to turn faucet handle on barrel
11. Pouring water (kinetic energy) tips plant pot into birdbath (gravity)
12. Displaced water (cause) flows through funnel (increased pressure) into waterwheel (effect)
13. Spinning waterwheel lifts gate (cause), releasing basketball toward upright books (effect)
14. Falling books (kinetic energy) strike chair rockers (potential energy)
15. Rocking chair (kinetic energy) taps car at the top of the ramp (potential energy)
16. Car taps balloon (cause), letting it rise (effect)
17. Rising balloon allows dog to see treat
18. Delighted dog wags tail (cause), drawing hairbrush across itchy back (effect) (accomplishing work)

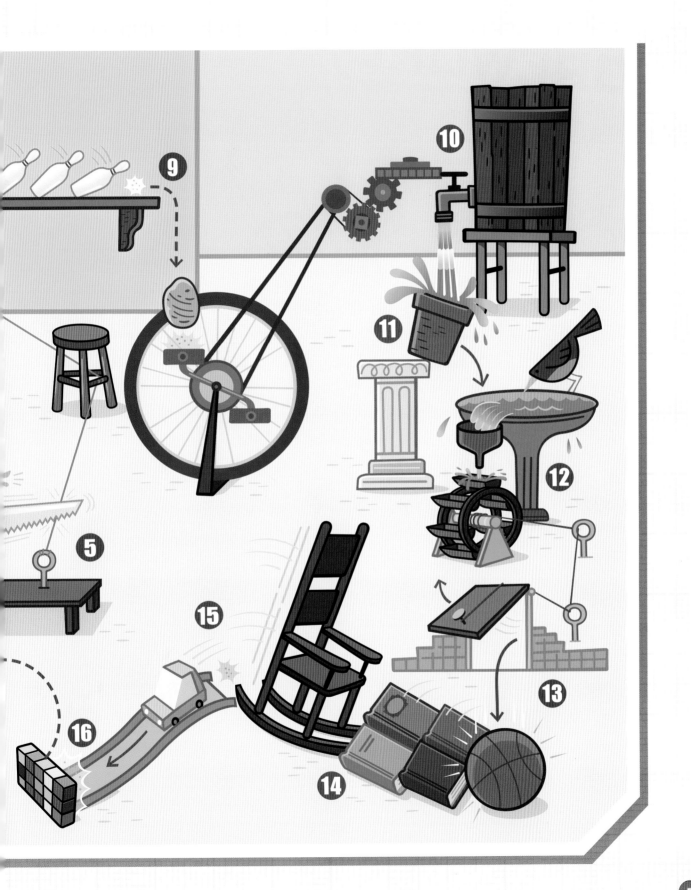

# FOREWORD

Back-Scratching Device

MACHINES OFTEN CONTAIN ENGINES, ELECTRONICS, AND A LOT OF MOVING PARTS, BUT NOT ALL OF THEM ARE THAT COMPLICATED. ANY TOOL DESIGNED TO PERFORM A TASK IS A MACHINE. **THE FIRST ENGINEERING BEGAN WITH SIX SIMPLE MACHINES WE STILL USE TODAY.** ONE OR MORE OF THESE ARE FOUND IN EVERY MECHANICAL OBJECT. THEY ALL HAVE THE SAME JOB—TO MAKE WORK EASIER. SIMPLE MACHINES ARE USED TO BUILD MORE COMPLICATED MACHINES, TO SOLVE HARDER PROBLEMS.

**CAN YOU SPOT THESE SIMPLE MACHINES** in the back-scratching device?

## Lever

THE LEVER IS USED TO LIFT OR MOVE OBJECTS THAT ARE HEAVY OR AWKWARD.

## Wheel and Axle

THE WHEEL AND AXLE IS USED TO CARRY LOADS WITH LITTLE EFFORT.

## Inclined Plane

THE INCLINED PLANE IS A FLAT SURFACE THAT IS HIGHER ON ONE END.

## Wedge

THE WEDGE IS A TOOL THAT CAN BE USED TO BREAK OBJECTS APART OR KEEP THEM TOGETHER.

## Pulley

THE PULLEY IS A WHEEL WITH A GROOVED RIM THAT HOLDS A ROPE.

THE SCREW IS AN INCLINED PLANE, MADE OF A CYLINDER WITH SPIRAL GROOVES.

## Screw

# ALL ABOUT ENGINEERING

Warning!
There are some hands-on experiments in here! Grab a grown-up and safety equipment!

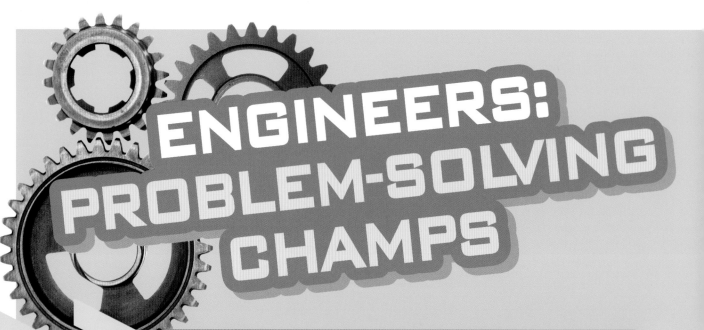

# ENGINEERS: PROBLEM-SOLVING CHAMPS

**HEY, HAVE YOU GOT A PROBLEM?** Most people face at least a few tricky situations throughout the day. Maybe your ball lands on the school roof and the only way to get it back is to find a way to climb a sheer wall. Suppose the chain on your bike breaks when you're far from home without any tools. Perhaps you're trying to enjoy some computer time on a laptop that keeps overheating.

Discovering the best solution might just mean finding an engineer—a person skilled at using math and science to overcome obstacles. Many engineers are specialists. They focus on a particular area such as mechanics, space, or computers. It often takes more than one kind of engineer to find a solution to a problem.

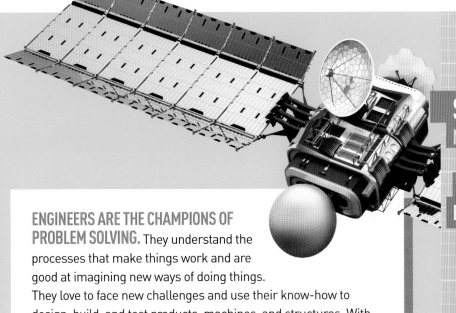

**ENGINEERS ARE THE CHAMPIONS OF PROBLEM SOLVING.** They understand the processes that make things work and are good at imagining new ways of doing things. They love to face new challenges and use their know-how to design, build, and test products, machines, and structures. With these kinds of skills, discovering the best way to scale a wall, fix a bike chain, and cool a computer isn't a problem—it's fun!

It's easy to see the many ways engineers impact the world. Just turn your head right, left, up, and down. Engineers design everything from floors and ceilings to fabrics, furniture, and food products. You can find them tackling issues deep underground, all over the Earth, and sky-high in outer space. Thanks to their ingenuity, we have different modes of transportation—bicycles, scooters, hovercraft, cars, trains, ships, planes, and spacecraft. We have smart buildings—houses, schools, hospitals, arenas, pools, and stadiums that use technology to automate and control different features. Engineers get credit for the machines we depend on, from toasters to car engines, elevators to tractors, and furnaces to freezers.

Fearless when it comes to facing jobs that have never before been tackled, engineers also work on big-world problems. They look for ways to provide people across the globe with access to clean water, sanitation, shelter, health care, nutritious crops, affordable energy, and safer roads. Their solutions make life easier and, more importantly, save lives. Engineers shape our world in the most amazing ways.

**SCIENTISTS** STUDY THE NATURAL WORLD **AND** TRY TO UNDERSTAND HOW IT WORKS. **THEY CONDUCT EXPERIMENTS AND DO RESEARCH TO FIGURE THINGS OUT.**

A SCIENTIST ASKS, "WHY DOES THIS HAPPEN?"

**WHAT'S THE DIFFERENCE** between a scientist and an engineer?

**ENGINEERS** USE SCIENCE AND MATH PRINCIPLES TO SOLVE PROBLEMS.

AN ENGINEER ASKS, "HOW CAN I FIX THIS OR MAKE IT BETTER?"

# WHOSE JOB IS THAT?

**MANY ENGINEERS ARE SPECIALISTS.** THEY FOCUS ON A PARTICULAR AREA, SUCH AS MECHANICS, SPACE, OR COMPUTERS. IT OFTEN TAKES **MORE THAN ONE KIND OF ENGINEER** TO FIND A SOLUTION TO A PROBLEM.

ENGINEERS HELP US **GET AROUND.**

**MECHANICAL ENGINEER**

**MARINE ENGINEER**

**AEROSPACE ENGINEER**

**CIVIL ENGINEER**

Marine engineers design water vehicles. They might make boats, ships, submarines, or aircraft carriers that are safer, more efficient, or longer lasting.

ENGINEERS GIVE US **PLACES TO LIVE** AND HANG OUT.

**CIVIL ENGINEER**

**MATERIALS ENGINEER**

**MECHANICAL ENGINEER**

**CHEMICAL ENGINEER**

**ELECTRONICS ENGINEER**

**COMPUTER SOFTWARE ENGINEER**

**MATERIALS ENGINEER**

**NUCLEAR ENGINEER**

**COMPUTER AND ELECTRICAL ENGINEER**

**ROBOTICS ENGINEER**

ENGINEERS FIGURE OUT HOW TO **MAKE THE PRODUCTS** WE NEED.

Robotics engineers design and build machines to do jobs for humans. Robots can do things that are too dangerous or difficult for people, like defusing a land mine, cleaning an oil spill, or exploring space.

ENGINEERS HELP **FEED US** AND **KEEP US HEALTHY.**

**AGRICULTURAL ENGINEER**

**BIOMEDICAL ENGINEER**

**CHEMICAL ENGINEER**

**INDUSTRIAL ENGINEER**

ENGINEERS WORK WITH **NATURAL RESOURCES.**

**ENVIRONMENTAL ENGINEER**

**GEOLOGICAL ENGINEER**

**PETROLEUM ENGINEER**

Petroleum engineers search for oil and natural gas beneath land and ocean. They might design extraction equipment, analyze discoveries in a lab, or explore ways to remove natural resources without harming the environment.

# FAMILY PORTRAIT

Imagine how it would look if everyone in your family was an engineer. Your grandparents and parents work in the traditional branches of engineering, but the rest of the family is all over the place, and some are into the newest technologies. Everyone's job involves designing, building, and testing, but each person has a different focus. This is how your family portrait might look.

## Where do you fit in the family tree?

Engineering includes dozens of main types, such as civil, electrical, and industrial, and even more subspecialties—areas that focus on specific areas of engineering. There are so many types of engineering to choose from and more new kinds developing all the time. Think about your interests and what kinds of problems you might like to solve. If you're not sure, the activities that follow are bound to give you some ideas.

**COUSIN LEVEE IS AN ENVIRONMENTAL ENGINEER.** He looks for ways to reduce pollution and make sure that natural resources, like water, are properly managed.

**GRAMPS IS A CIVIL ENGINEER.** He designs big construction projects. Gramps has lived so long, it's hard to find a road, tunnel, dam, or bridge he didn't help develop, test, or maintain.

**GRANDMA IS A CHEMICAL ENGINEER.** She finds ways to use chemicals in foods, medicines, fuels, and other valuable products.

**POPSY IS AN INDUSTRIAL ENGINEER.** He figures out how to improve things that already exist by making them more efficient and safe.

**GRANNY IS AN ELECTRICAL ENGINEER.** She finds ways to use electrical energy in the design of motors, radar equipment, power plants, and other systems.

**AUNT SKYLAR IS AN AEROSPACE ENGINEER.** She knows how to design and build machines that fly, such as aircraft, spacecraft, drones, and rockets.

**MOM IS A MATERIALS ENGINEER**—an expert on how ceramics (like clay or quartz), metals (like copper and nickel), polymers (like plastics and glue), and composites (like wood and concrete) respond to processing.

**DAD IS A GEOLOGICAL ENGINEER.** He searches for mineral deposits and designs mines to access coal and metals in the ground.

**AUNT MILLI IS A NUCLEAR ENGINEER** who works on finding ways to use nuclear energy and radiation. She used to study how nuclear energy can be used to power ships and spacecraft, but now she focuses on how it can be used in medicine.

**UNCLE ARCHIE IS A BIOMEDICAL ENGINEER.** His job is to create technologies for health care. He's developed medical instruments and machines, and even artificial organs and prosthetics—devices to replace body parts that are missing or not working.

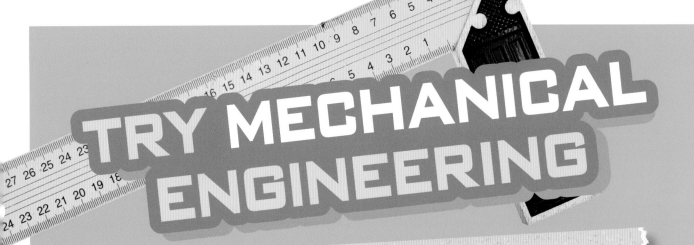

# TRY MECHANICAL ENGINEERING

## Have a Blast With Water

## WHAT YOU NEED

>> 5/8-inch (1.6-cm) (outside diameter) wooden dowel, 16 inches (40.6 cm)

>> 3/4-inch (1.9-cm) (inside diameter) PVC pipe, 12 inches (30.5 cm)

>> pushpin

>> soda bottle cap (A cap lined with a flat plastic seal inside works best.)

>> duct tape

>> bucket filled with water

## WHAT TO DO

**1** Use the pushpin to carefully make a hole though the center of the bottle cap.

**2** Place the cap on the end of the pipe and tape it firmly in place.

**3** Wrap about 10 layers of duct tape around one end of the dowel's circumference.

**4** Push the taped end of the dowel into the pipe. If you can't feel any resistance as it slides through the pipe, add more tape. If it's hard to push, remove tape until it fits well enough to move without pushing too hard.

**5** Place the cap end of the blaster into the bucket of water. Fill the pipe with water by pulling all but 2–3 inches (5–8 cm) of the dowel out of the pipe.

**6** Go outside where nothing can be ruined by getting wet. Aim the blaster at a thirsty tree and push the stick firmly into the pipe.

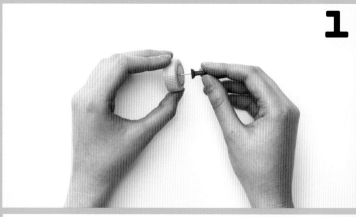

**1**

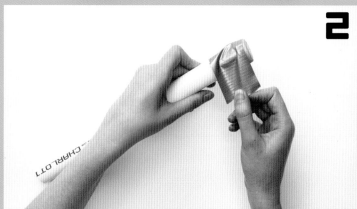

**2**

**3**

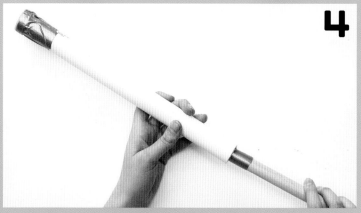

**4**

Under normal conditions, most liquids, including water, cannot be compressed—squished into a smaller space. That's why juice squirts out the straw when you squeeze a juice box. Water inside the blaster responds to pressure in the same way. It can't fit into a smaller space, so when you make its space smaller, it escapes. The harder you push, the faster the water will shoot out.

> **ENGINEERS CAN USE THE POWER OF MOVING LIQUIDS TO EXERT FORCE. MACHINES THAT USE THE MOTION OF LIQUIDS TO DO WORK ARE CALLED HYDRAULICS.**

Let's break that down.

**1.** The water inside your blaster is stored in the PVC pipe.

**2.** The dowel sliding into the pipe acts as a pump, creating pressure.

**3.** When you force the wooden stick into the pipe, pressure builds because the water cannot compress.

**4.** Water shoots out the hole!

## YOUR JOB AS A MECHANICAL ENGINEER

Consider how you can improve the design. How might you alter the blaster to carry more water, shoot water farther or faster, or make the pipe easier to grip?

# TRY ACOUSTIC ENGINEERING

## Make Some Beautiful Music

## WHAT YOU NEED

>> 2 tongue depressors (or large craft sticks)

>> 1 old greeting card or file folder cut into two 1/2 x 3–inch (1.5 x 8–cm) strips

>> 1 wide rubber band, long enough to stay in place when wrapped the length of the stick

>> 2 small rubber bands, small enough to wrap around the width of the sticks

>> tape

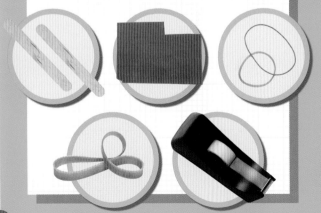

## WHAT TO DO

**1** Place one stick on top of the other.

**2** About a half inch from the sticks' end, make a paper loop by wrapping a paper strip around the wood. Tape the paper loop together, being careful not to tape the paper to the sticks.

**3** Repeat on the other end of the sticks.

**4** Remove one stick by gently pulling it out to the side. Stretch the wide rubber band along the length of the stick with the paper rings.

**5** Place the second stick on top of the rubber band.

**6** Wrap the small rubber bands around the paper loops to hold both sticks together.

**7** Test your harmonica by holding the two ends, then blowing and inhaling through the sticks to make different sounds.

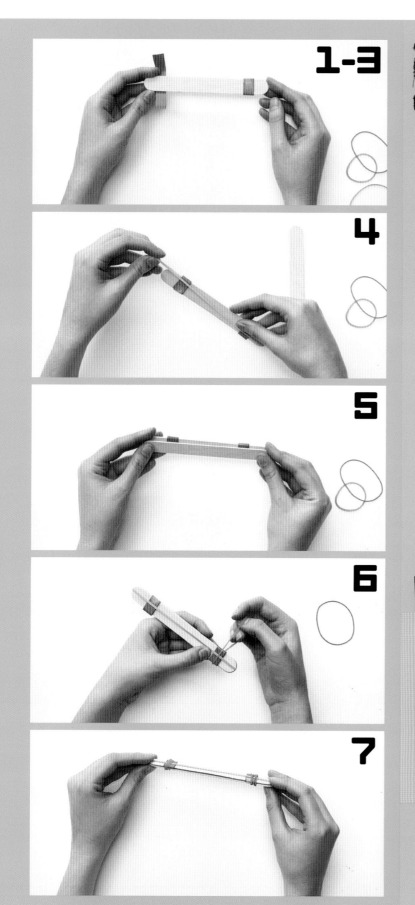

**1-3**

**4**

**5**

**6**

**7**

You know sound is something you hear, but did you know it's always caused by the vibration of air? Sound travels in compression waves. The more the waves are squeezed together, the louder the sound. When you blow through the harmonica, moving air makes the rubber band vibrate, creating a compression wave—the sound you hear. The number of times per second the rubber band vibrates determines its frequency. Blowing harder creates a greater frequency and higher note; blowing softly creates a decreased frequency and lower note. The rubber band's thickness also affects frequency.

> YOU CAN TALK AND SING BECAUSE YOU HAVE VOCAL CORDS THAT MAKE SOUND BY VIBRATING AIR.

## YOUR JOB AS AN ACOUSTIC ENGINEER

Experiment with other materials to create harmonicas that play different notes. What happens if you use rubber bands or pieces of paper that are thicker or thinner? Try using ice pop sticks, paint stir sticks, or short rulers, and compare your results.

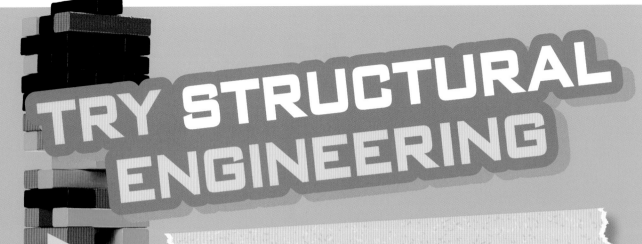

## Presto Chango: Make a Paper Cup

## WHAT YOU NEED

>> 8-inch (20-cm) square each of waxed paper, newspaper, and printer paper

**THE JAPANESE ART OF PAPER FOLDING, CALLED ORIGAMI,** is inspiring engineers to look at their designs in new ways. It's a step toward understanding how other materials could be bent to make them stronger, smaller, and flatter. For example, building paper prototypes, or models, helps engineers explore strengths and weaknesses of designs. Folding can help aeronautic engineers send materials into space, automotive engineers design air bags, and biomedical engineers create health devices for use inside the human body.

## WHAT TO DO

**1** Lay one piece of paper on a table so that the square is a diamond shape, with the points up and down, left and right. Fold the right point to the left to form a triangle.

**2** With the new triangle pointing to the left, fold the bottom point up to align with the top left edge.

**3** Fold the top point down so that it aligns with the previous fold.

**4** Rotate the paper so that the point is at the top. Fold one flap of the point down.

**5** Flip the cup over and fold down the other flap.

**6** Open the cup.

**7** Pour in some water to check out how water-tight it is!

**8** Repeat with the other types of paper to test which holds water the longest.

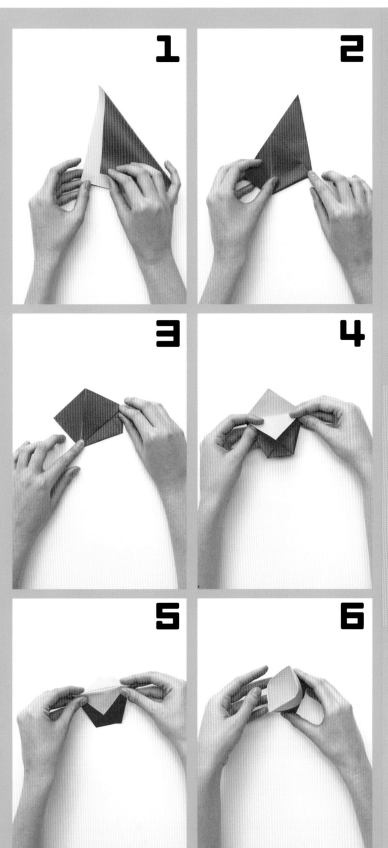

## 1

## 2

## 3

## 4

## 5

## 6

## 7

# What's Happening

Paper is a porous material. Its empty spaces allow water to seep through it. Newspaper is more porous than printer paper, so water escapes through it more quickly. Wax is not a porous material, so waxed paper prevents water from seeping through the cup.

**CREASES ADD STRESS TO THE PAPER, MAKING IT WEAKER, BUT THE FOLDED SHAPE STRENGTHENS THE CUP BY SPREADING THE WEIGHT OF THE LOAD.**

## YOUR JOB AS A STRUCTURAL ENGINEER

What other materials can you fold into a cup? Try aluminum foil, a cloth napkin, parchment paper, or wallpaper. What happens if you make cups out of larger or smaller squares of paper? Can you think of other uses for your creations? Observe how the cups respond to holding different liquids, such as pancake syrup, liquid soap, or ketchup.

# HOW ENGINEERS SOLVE PROBLEMS

## The Engineering Process

YOU MIGHT SEE A TOUGH PROBLEM AND THINK, **"OH NO! NOW WHAT?"** AN ENGINEER FACING THE SAME PROBLEM MIGHT THINK, "HA, HA! **A CHALLENGE! WHAT FUN!** I'M GOING TO SOLVE THIS! NOW HOW CAN I BREAK THIS PROBLEM INTO STEPS?"

**ENGINEERS FOLLOW A SERIES OF STEPS TO FIND THE BEST SOLUTION TO A PROBLEM.** These steps, called the engineering process, are: define the problem, brainstorm, pick your best idea, design, build, test, revise, and share results.

Engineers typically start by following the steps in the order shown. Sometimes, though, they make discoveries along the way that call for design changes and the need to repeat certain steps. It's common for engineers to overcome problems that occur along the way by redesigning, rebuilding, and retesting. This approach is known as iteration—the action of repeating a series of steps to get closer to a solution. Engineers will redo the steps as many times as necessary. Although the middle steps may be repeated, the process always begins with defining the problem. And if all goes well, it ends with a solution.

# THE PROCESS

**STEP 1: DEFINE THE PROBLEM**

**STEP 2: BRAINSTORM**

**STEP 3: PICK YOUR BEST IDEA**

**STEP 4: DESIGN**

**STEP 5: BUILD**

**STEP 6: TEST**

**STEP 7: REVISE**

**STEP 8: SHARE RESULTS**

>> # DEFINE THE PROBLEM

*Step One*

## THE FIRST STEP IS TO CLEARLY DEFINE THE PROBLEM.

You need to know: What's wrong? What problem needs to be solved? Stating your problem clearly means breaking it down into one *solvable* question. And it lays out the criteria for success. For example, suppose your sister placed your favorite book just out of reach. The problem isn't just, "How can I get the book off the superhigh shelf?" It's, "How can I get the book off the superhigh shelf without getting hurt and with only the resources I can find in this house?"

**Problem:**
HOW CAN I RETRIEVE A BOOK FROM A TALL BOOKSHELF **WITHOUT GETTING HURT AND** ONLY USING THINGS AVAILABLE TO ME IN THE HOUSE?

>> *Step Two*

# BRAINSTORM

## PROBLEM SOLVING BEGINS WITH BRAINSTORMING.

It sounds like a hurricane spinning inside your head. Like a storm, it's unpredictable, but it can also be wildly fun! All you need to do is:

>> Think about the problem.
>> Write down every possible solution.
>> Don't judge the ideas!

The key is to think of as many ideas as you can without worrying about what will or won't work. There are no wrong answers at this point. Why? Because even crazy suggestions can take you in a useful direction. Ideas flow better when you stop yourself from pointing out the impossible. Goofy ideas can lead to gems, so leave the judging for later. Each idea will lead to another, so the more you list, the more creative your thoughts will become. You can brainstorm alone, but it's even more fun with a group. Warning: It can be a noisy affair. Get one person to make a list while everyone blurts out solutions.

### Possible Solutions

Retrieve the book!

- Stand on a chair to reach the top of the bookshelf.
- Ask a tall person for help.
- Borrow a ladder from a neighbor.
- Lasso the book and pull it down.
- Knock the book down with a broom.
- Place a remote control car on top of the shelf and nudge the book over the edge.
- Use a remote control helicopter to drop a loop of string around the book and bring it down.

- Buy, rent, or borrow a parrot and train it to retrieve objects.
- Stack bricks and wood to make a staircase to the shelf.
- Stick chewed bubble gum on the end of a yardstick, touch it to the book, and pull the book down.
- Make a human pyramid high enough for the top person to reach the book.
- Build a robotic hand that can grasp the book and pass it down.
- Make a vacuum hose extension out of cardboard and use suction to get the book down.

# PICK YOUR BEST IDEA

**Step Three**

## NOW YOU GET TO JUDGE EACH IDEA.

One way to do that is to make a chart and sort each idea into a category: yes, no, or maybe. Rather than dismissing an idea as impossible, stay positive by questioning whether the idea can be improved.

Asking questions will help you choose the best solution. You may know the answers or you may need to do some research. You might consider, "Is this idea safe? How long will it take? Do I have the materials I will need? How much will this cost?"

Answering questions helps you define your design criteria—how you will judge whether a solution is likely to be successful. You will also need to consider design constraints—what could prevent each solution from working?

In this situation, you could sum up your criteria for success this way:

MY SOLUTION WILL ALLOW ME TO GET MY BOOK DOWN **WITHIN TWO HOURS, WITHOUT HURTING MYSELF OR WRECKING ANYTHING** IN THE HOUSE.

Retrieve the book!

# PROJECT: OPERATION BOOK RESCUE

After you fill out the chart, review your "maybe" answers to choose the best approach.

| IDEA | NO | MAYBE | RATIONALE |
|---|:---:|:---:|---|
| Stand on a chair to reach the top of the bookshelf. | ✘ | | CONSTRAINT: Chair not sturdy enough.<br>CONCLUSION: Unsafe and I still wouldn't be able to reach. |
| Ask a tall person for help. | | ✘ | CONSTRAINT: My brother is tall, but he's at a friend's house.<br>CONCLUSION: He's never home when I need him. |
| Borrow a ladder from a neighbor. | | ✘ | CONSTRAINT: Neighbor will ask why I need a ladder.<br>CONCLUSION: Talking with my neighbor will take too long. |
| Lasso the book and pull it down. | ✘ | | CONSTRAINT: I would need to practice for months.<br>CONCLUSION: I need to find a solution that takes less time. |
| Knock the book down with a broom. | | ✘ | CONSTRAINT: Risk of breaking things.<br>CONCLUSION: Find a safer solution. |
| Place a remote control car on top of the shelf and nudge the book over the edge. | ✘ | | CONSTRAINT: I can't reach high enough to put the car in place. It might land upside down if I throw it.<br>CONCLUSION: Find a less risky solution. |
| Use a remote control helicopter to drop a loop of string around the book and bring it down. | ✘ | | CONSTRAINT: Materials not available. Too expensive to borrow. High risk of damaging helicopter.<br>CONCLUSION: Too complicated. |
| Buy, rent, or borrow a parrot and train it to retrieve objects. | ✘ | | CONSTRAINT: Allergy to birds will make me swell like a balloon. Also, it would take a long time to train a bird.<br>CONCLUSION: Don't involve an animal. |
| Stack bricks and wood to make a stair-case to the cupboard. | | ✘ | CONSTRAINT: Probably couldn't gather materials soon enough.<br>CONCLUSION: Find solution that only needs household items. |
| Stick chewed bubble gum on the end of a yardstick, touch it to the book, and pull it down. | | ✘ | CONSTRAINT: I only have one piece of sugar-free gum.<br>CONCLUSION: It won't be big or gooey enough. However, if I could find more gum in the house, this might work. |
| Make a human pyramid high enough for the top person to reach the book. | ✘ | | CONSTRAINT: A pyramid that high would take a lot of people.<br>CONCLUSION: I could be crushed. It would take too long to find enough people. |
| Build a robotic hand that can grasp the book and pass it down. | | ✘ | CONSTRAINT: It would take me a really long time to design and build.<br>CONCLUSION: This could work if I didn't need my book right away. |
| Make a vacuum hose extension out of card-board and use suction to get the book down. | | ✘ | CONSTRAINT: None.<br>CONCLUSION: Materials available. Fastest solution. |

# >> DESIGN  Step Four

## ENGINEERING INVOLVES THINKING ABOUT MANY DIFFERENT APPROACHES BEFORE PICKING THE BEST ONE.

The more work you do on paper, the less you need to do when you reach the building stage. Begin by listing materials, keeping in mind your constraint—to only use objects that can be found around the house. You've already decided to use cardboard, but what kind would work best? You know corrugated cardboard is too thick and inflexible. Poster board would be easier to cut and bend, but you don't have any. Then you remember this morning's breakfast came out of a jumbo cereal box. You add "large cereal box" to your list, along with "scissors" to cut it. Knowing you need a way to attach the cardboard to the vacuum hose, you write down "masking tape." It's handy—right here in the kitchen drawer—and you don't think clear tape would be strong enough. Looking up at the shelf, you realize the cardboard won't be long enough to reach that high, so you add "chair" to your list, and of course, "vacuum cleaner."

>> **Next, draw a picture to show how your solution will look.** Your first drawings will be rough drafts. It can take many tries to get a design the way you want it, but redrawing helps prevent problems during testing.

>> **As you draw, predict how your materials will interact with one another by identifying their characteristics and examining cause-and-effect relationships.** For example, the vacuum hose is flexible. Will it bend too much when you extend it upward? The book is made up of many pieces of paper. Will the vacuum have enough power to grab it?

>> **If you identify problems within your design, consider the variables—the parts that can be changed.** Testing the effects of changing a single variable at a time allows you to see how one solution works compared to another. You can't change the weight of the book—that's not a variable. But you might be able to find a way to stop the hose from bending—that *is* a variable.

>> **After your design is complete, estimate costs and list the steps needed to build the invention.** Your instructions should be clear enough for anyone to follow. This allows others to test your design, suggest improvements, and solve the problem, too.

Retrieve the book!

## PROJECT: OPERATION BOOK RESCUE

## SKETCH
An early draft of your vacuum–cereal box solution might start out looking like this:

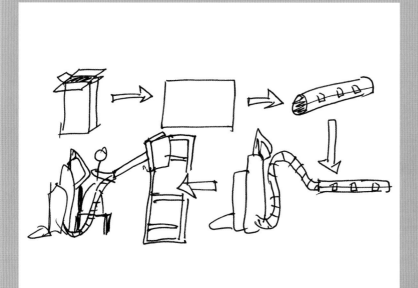

A final draft might look more like this:

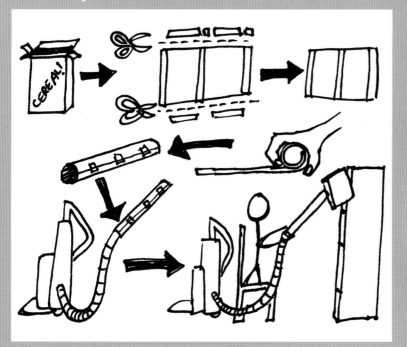

## MATERIALS
Large cereal box
Masking tape
Vacuum cleaner
Chair

## TOOLS
Scissors

## COSTS
None. Items can be found around the home.

## STEPS
**1** Unfold a jumbo-size cereal box to form a single flat piece of cardboard.
**2** Cut the excess flaps of cardboard away to form a large rectangle.
**3** Roll the cardboard into a tube.
**4** Tape the cardboard together to make the tube hold its shape.
**5** Attach the tube to the end of the vacuum and tape it in place.

By adjusting only one variable at a time, you will know the cause of any change you observe.

# BUILD

## Step Five

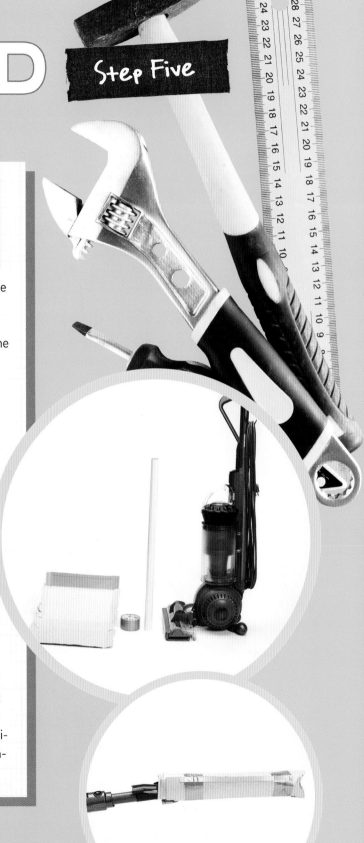

**BECAUSE YOU'VE OUTLINED YOUR DESIGN SO CLEARLY,** YOU KNOW EXACTLY WHAT TO DO WHEN YOU GET READY TO BUILD YOUR SOLUTION.

Still, surprises and setbacks are normal. Suppose the cereal box creases when you try to roll it. You might have to adjust your design as you go along. That's okay because your plan is a guideline that you created to organize your process. If better ideas occur to you, feel free to explore them, as long as they meet your criteria to solve the problem.

As you build, you might notice something funny. Working with tools and materials can trigger new ideas. Holding the cardboard in your hands, you might wonder if toilet paper rolls would work better, but they're so short. Could you tape a few together? A paper towel roll is longer, but flimsy. Digging through the recycling bin, you find an empty box of aluminum foil with a thick, sturdy roll inside. A colorful piece of paper is caught in the box. Eureka! It makes you think of using a wrapping paper roll.

Attaching the cardboard roll to the vacuum is not as easy as you thought. The masking tape isn't sticky or wide enough to do a good job. You substitute duct tape and your vacuum extension is complete. Now it's time to see how well it works.

# TEST

*Step Six*

## THIS IS THE BIG MOMENT. WILL YOUR PROTO-TYPE WORK OR WILL TESTING SHOW YOU NEED TO MODIFY IT?

1. Plug in and turn on the vacuum.
2. Stand on the chair.
3. Push the hose extension up to the book.
4. Retrieve the book.

Ready, set, go! You turn on the vacuum, but before you can even climb onto the chair, a horrible sucking sound makes you freeze. Your eyes turn to the noise and you see the tube's end is collapsed. You also see a correlation—a relationship between two variables—between the suction and the cardboard. The cardboard is not strong enough to hold its shape against the powerful force of a household vacuum. Now what?

# REVISE

*Step Seven*

## STEP SEVEN IS ALL ABOUT INVESTIGATING YOUR RESULTS TO ANALYZE WHAT DID AND DIDN'T WORK.

Look at what you've done and consider how you can make it better. The good news is the duct tape kept everything in place. All you need is a weaker vacuum, a sturdier tube, or a way to make your tube stronger.

It seems engineering is a bit like a board game. You might go in a straight line from start to finish or you might need to take a few steps back and try again. Sometimes you have to revise your model, and this is one of those times.

You return to the design stage and decide to attach the sturdy aluminum foil roll to the end of the cardboard tube. To keep it from flopping about, you tape chopsticks around the joint. Once rebuilding is complete, you test your invention, and this time it works. Not only have you successfully practiced engineering, you've got your book back thanks to a novel idea.

# SHARE RESULTS

**Step Eight**

## ON THE JOB, ENGINEERS SHARE THEIR RESULTS WITH CO-WORKERS.

They might write a report or create a presentation that shows how their solution works, as well as what went wrong. Writing about mistakes helps engineers pinpoint errors and figure out how to prevent similar problems from happening again. Recording setbacks helps other people avoid making the same mistakes. Talking about what happened can trigger new problem-solving ideas, such as how to make the invention faster or with cheaper materials.

Why not share your data around the supper table? AN OUTLINE FOR YOUR DISCUSSION MIGHT LOOK LIKE THIS:

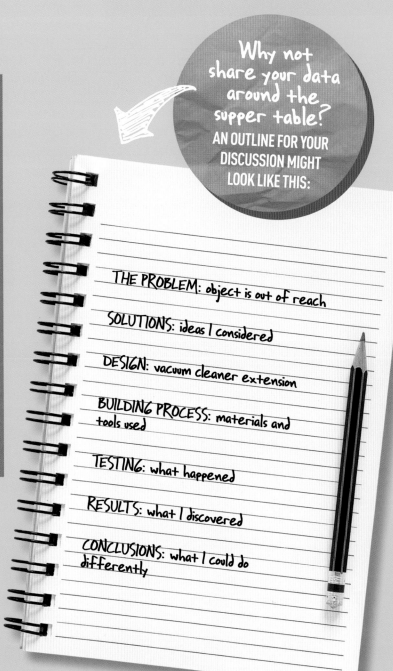

THE PROBLEM: object is out of reach

SOLUTIONS: ideas I considered

DESIGN: vacuum cleaner extension

BUILDING PROCESS: materials and tools used

TESTING: what happened

RESULTS: what I discovered

CONCLUSIONS: what I could do differently

## THINK YOU'RE UP TO THE CHALLENGE OF ENGINEERING? BEFORE YOU DIVE IN, DO SOME PLANNING WITH THIS HANDY PROJECT PLANNING CHECKLIST.

## PROJECT:

○ **DEFINE THE PROBLEM**

○ **LIST POSSIBLE SOLUTIONS**

○ **SELECT THE BEST IDEA**

○ **DESCRIBE THE DESIGN**

List materials

List tools

Show costs

Sketch design

List building steps

○ **BUILD**

List modifications made during building process

○ **TEST**

Describe testing method and results

○ **REVISE**

Describe changes made after testing

○ **SHARE RESULTS**

Write down what you discovered

Instead of writing in the book, photocopy this page so you'll have a template you can copy again and again.

# SOLVE THIS!

Warning!
There are awesome challenges and solutions inside. Be safe, grab a grown-up, and get your hands dirty!

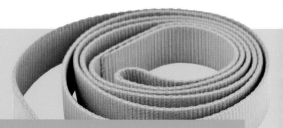

## IMAGINE A DARE AND DOUBLE DARE ROLLED INTO ONE.
### *SOLVE THIS!* IS LIKE A GAME SHOW CHALLENGE. PLAYERS MUST CRACK TOUGH PROBLEMS WITH BRAND-NEW SOLUTIONS.

Who is brave enough to take such a dare? Hopefully you! But you don't need to go it alone. Take the challenges alongside National Geographic Explorers and engineers—leaders and go-getters who inspire others with their creative thinking. They have experience overcoming obstacles and the kind of attitudes that holler, "We can do it! Let's keep trying! There must be a way!" The Explorers are known for going on problem-solving adventures. Can *Solve This!* stump these smarty-pants? Let's find out.

## HOW IT WORKS

The challenge takers—and yes, that includes you!—must follow five rules.

1. The problem must be solved **within 24 hours.**
2. The solution should **use everyday materials** that are readily available.
3. Ordinary hand tools may be used but **power tools are not allowed.**
4. You can **work alone or with friends.**
5. The solution must be reached **following the steps of engineering:**

1. Define the problem
2. Brainstorm
3. Pick the best idea
4. Design
5. Build
6. Test
7. Revise
8. Share results

# MEET THE
# SOLUTION PANEL

YOU'LL BE ATTEMPTING THE CHALLENGES ALONG WITH THESE NATIONAL GEOGRAPHIC SUPERSTARS. CAN THEY FIGURE OUT A SOLUTION TO THE CHALLENGES? FIND OUT ON THE PAGES FOLLOWING EACH CHALLENGE.*

**MEET THE EXPLORERS:** National Geographic Explorers are scientists, engineers, innovators, and inventors. From diving with sharks to summiting mountains to exploring distant planets, they face some of the toughest challenges. You never know what you'll be facing in the field, so quick thinking and creative solutions can save the day.

### CONSTANCE ADAMS, *Space Architect*

Hi, I'm Constance. I am a space architect. My job is to design and build habitats that make it possible for people to live in space. I've worked on space shuttle design and the International Space Station. One of my projects has been to work with others to create an inflatable habitat for humans on a mission to Mars. The habitat has to be small enough to launch but large enough for people to work in and live comfortably.

### MUNAZZA ALAM, *Astronomer*

Hi, I'm Munazza. I'm an astronomer and graduate student. My work has involved research in both the astrophysics department and at a natural history museum! To collect data, I've used telescopes in Arizona and Hawaii, U.S.A., and in Chile. I've worked with the Hubble Space Telescope, too. I want to understand what weather is like on planets beyond our solar system.

### RYAN EAGLESON, *Coral Reef Biologist*

Hi, I'm Ryan. I'm a coral reef biologist using underwater remotely operated vehicles (ROVs) to find better ways to protect coral reefs. My interest in coral reefs began with a love of turtles that led to an obsession with oceans. One of my projects was to look at mustard hill coral and other corals that are able to survive okay in disturbed environments, such as hurricane-damaged areas, where other corals were dying.

*Note! These explorers and engineers are professionals. Check with an adult before trying out any of their solutions.

### DENISE POZZI-ESCOT, Archaeologist

Hi, I'm Denise. I study South American archaeology, specifically pre-Columbian cultures (which were in the Americas before Europeans arrived in 1492). I've studied and been a professor in Peru and in France, and I'm director at the Pachacamac Site Museum. The site includes pyramids and homes from past cultures in this area of what is now Peru. We have lots of artifacts here, too. This site was inhabited as far back as A.D. 200!

### CINDY LIUTKUS-PIERCE, Geologist

Hi, I'm Cindy. I am a geologist and college professor who studies ancient sediments to reconstruct past environments. Each summer, I travel all over the world to collect rock samples, find fossils, and explore remote places. I want to figure out how Earth's changing environments affected human evolution, even back to our primate ancestors.

### ERIKA BERGMAN, Deep-Sea Submersible Pilot

Hi, I'm Erika. I pilot submarines and underwater drones. I've always loved to fix broken machines and tools, figure out how cameras work and take photos, and adventure down the beach or into the woods to test out my new inventions and skills. I love to explore new places, either by land or by sea. The latest technology helps me go deeper, see farther, and learn more about my favorite places.

### JEFF MARLOW, Geobiologist

Hi, I'm Jeff. I'm a geobiologist, a job that allows me to study microorganisms in extreme locations around the world. I visit the deep ocean and active volcanoes to learn more about how these microbes survive in such crazy conditions and shape our planet. My work explores how microorganisms could be used to generate biofuels and other useful products for society, or how they could tell us more about the possibility of life on other planets.

### CECILIA MAURICIO, Archaeologist

Hi, I'm Cecilia. I'm an archaeologist in Peru. I specialize in environmental studies in pre-Columbian archaeology. I study the role that climate and environment played in big social transformations. For example, I look at how changes in the climate contributed to the rise and fall of civilizations, and how farming changed the biodiversity of forests.

# MEET THE ENGINEERS: National Geographic's intrepid engineers work in their lab and in the field to aid the Explorers, photographers, and staff of National Geographic. From building wildfire-proof camera cases and camera collars for lions to sending drones soaring, they work together to develop incredible, creative solutions for any challenge thrown their way.

**ERIC BERKENPAS**
Senior Director,
National Geographic
Remote Imaging

**TOM O'BRIEN**
Photo Engineer, *National Geographic* Magazine

**MIKE SHEPARD**
Mechanical Engineer,
National Geographic
Remote Imaging

**BRAD HENNING**
Electrical Engineer,
National Geographic
Remote Imaging

And meet me, too!

**JOAN, Author**

I'm Joan, and I'm the author. When it came time to add a few of my own solutions, a tiny finger of fear poked at my heart. I create problems; I don't solve them. Ask anyone! Could I rise to my own challenges? Could I overcome that I-don't-know-where-to-start feeling? It turns out I could! Following the engineering process was all it took to get me unstuck. Many of its steps are the same ones I use when writing books—brainstorm, choose the best idea, and revise. All it takes is practice. No fear here!

# THE CHALLENGE

## MUFFLE THE PARTY

### OBJECTIVE: SOUNDPROOF YOUR BEDROOM BEFORE TONIGHT'S SLEEPOVER

## The Situation

Your best friend is coming for a sleepover and you plan to stay awake all night. Unfortunately, your buddy doesn't have an indoor voice. How can you soundproof your bedroom with items around the house and still make it look like a cool place to hang out?

SOLUTIONS! >>

# SOLUTIONS

Challenge #1: Soundproof Your Bedroom Before Tonight's Sleepover

>> STUFFY SOLUTION

**MUNAZZA**
Astronomer

### DESCRIBE YOUR SOLUTION.

To soundproof my room, I'd use stuffed animals, blankets, and pillows. The first order of business would be to take care of the door. It likely has gaps in the side and bottom where sound will escape the most, so I'd need to cover those up. I'd drape a blanket over the door (for a tentlike/clubhouse feel) and make a stuffed animal chain to frame the doorway. I'd line up my pillows on the walls bordering the bunk bed so that our voices would be muted if we decided to talk as we fell asleep. For extra soundproofing, I could hang a blanket on the remaining wall to further muffle the sounds of our voices.

### WHAT WAS YOUR FIRST IDEA?

The first image that pops in my mind when I think of a soundproof room is one with soft, squishy foam padding on the walls, just like in recording studios! So I modeled my solution on what I could similarly construct based on items I could likely find in my room.

### WHAT WERE YOUR CRITERIA FOR A SUCCESSFUL SOLUTION?

My solution required the use of materials that would absorb or deflect the noise coming from inside the room. Soundproofing equipment is generally soft/thick and made from materials like foam, so I tried to incorporate similar items in my solution.

# FANTASTIC FORT

CINDY
Geologist

**DESCRIBE YOUR SOLUTION.**

The main problem is to find the best way to either deaden any sound or keep my friend quiet. Since my friend is bound to resist any serious methods for shushing, it's easier to deaden the sound. I would build a fort out of mattresses, couch cushions, pillows, and blankets. These items would absorb sound and the fort would be a cool place to spend the night while we stay up and talk. My friend would never know my ulterior motive.

**HOW COULD YOUR SOLUTION BE USED FOR A REAL-WORLD PROBLEM?**

This solution is a very common way to deaden sound. It's used in restaurants where there is a lot of noise from people talking. Putting panels of material on the ceiling of the restaurant helps to keep the noise levels down.

# MASTER MUFFLER

JEFF
Geobiologist

**DESCRIBE YOUR SOLUTION.**

The sound waves traveling from my friend's mouth must be stopped from reaching my parents' ears. The sound can be blocked anywhere along the path it travels. We can focus on the source (my friend's mouth), or the end point (my parents' ears), or anywhere in between. My solution is to ask my friend to wear a mask that muffles his voice! Dressing up like an alien or a monster would add some fun to the night as well.

**WHY DID YOU CHOOSE THESE SPECIFIC MATERIALS AND TOOLS?**

I would need a good mask for my friend—one that is breathable but still muffles the voice effectively. The benefit is that it's simple—we just need one item to solve the problem! The downside is that my friend might not want to wear a scary mask all night.

**HOW COULD YOUR SOLUTION BE USED FOR A REAL-WORLD PROBLEM?**

Muffling sound by going to the source of the sound, rather than trying to block it after it has already been emitted, could be useful for a lot of loud machines, like airplane engines, lawn mowers, leaf blowers, or cars. Wrapping the motors with something to soak up the sound or building them with quieter, lower-friction parts in the first place would make cities a nicer place to live!

More Solutions

# NAT GEO ENGINEER
# SOLUTIONS

THE NAT GEO ENGINEERS REALLY CAUGHT THE WAVE—THE SOUND WAVE!—IN THESE SOLUTIONS.

Challenge #1: Soundproof Your Bedroom Before Tonight's Sleepover

ERIC

So, the problem is that the sound will echo in the room and eventually make its way out. We need to scatter and absorb the energy of the sound before it escapes.

THE BLANKET PARTLY SCATTERS SOUND BUT MOSTLY ABSORBS IT.

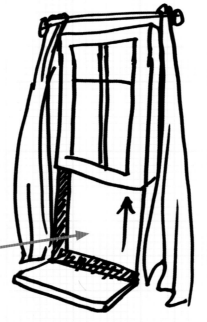

AN OPEN WINDOW HELPS SOUND ESCAPE.

You could open the windows to let the sound pressure out and place a blanket against the crack of the door to absorb sound.

TOM

# THE CHALLENGE

## SWEET SECURITY

### OBJECTIVE: PROTECT YOUR CANDY STASH

THINGS THAT MAKE NOISE COULD EITHER SCARE THE THIEF OR ALERT YOU!

## The Situation

It happens all the time. You go in your room and something's off. Maybe your sock isn't draped across your backpack the way you left it or the books on your desk are at odd angles. You go straight to your candy stash, and sure enough, almost all the bubble gum is missing. How can you stop the thief?

STRING COULD BE USEFUL FOR RIGGING SOMETHING UP.

SOLUTIONS!

## Challenge #2: Protect Your Candy Stash

### SNEAKY SOLUTION

**CINDY**
*Geologist*

### DESCRIBE YOUR SOLUTION.

Dust flour on the floor near the candy stash. Anyone stepping into the flour will leave a footprint, and you could catch the individual by looking at the print size or shoe type. You could also identify the thief by checking your family's shoes for traces of powder. My father used to joke about doing this to my sister and me on Christmas Eve, to make sure we wouldn't go downstairs and see our presents before Christmas morning!

### WHY DID YOU CHOOSE THESE SPECIFIC MATERIALS AND TOOLS?

It's easy! You could use anything around the house that would accept a footprint, like flour or baby powder. This solution uses a principle in forensic science known as the exchange principle—two things that come into contact leave traces upon one another.

### HOW COULD YOUR SOLUTION BE USED FOR A REAL-WORLD PROBLEM?

Footprint recognition is often used in forensic science as a means to identify suspects in criminal cases. Dusting for fingerprints, which is similar to dusting for footprints, is also a great way to identify suspects.

# MAGIC MIRROR

RYAN
Coral Reef Biologist

## DESCRIBE YOUR SOLUTION.

My plan is to place mirrors in the jar of bubble gum to give the illusion that the container is empty, even though in reality, it is as full as I left it. This is much like the method magicians use to make boxes look empty during their tricks. Mirrors would probably be needed on three sides of the container, with one mirror facing the thief's direction.

## WHY DID YOU CHOOSE THESE SPECIFIC MATERIALS AND TOOLS?

At first, I considered what tools would be best for cutting the mirrors into certain angles to make the trick most believable. In the end, I decided using three or four correctly sized mirrors was the easiest choice as long as they could be placed correctly to maintain the illusion. If not concealed properly and someone picked up the container, the trick would be uncovered!

## HOW COULD YOUR SOLUTION BE USED FOR A REAL-WORLD PROBLEM?

This could be a quick solution for hiding something valuable in plain sight without many materials or expensive tools such as cameras or motion detectors. Mirror setups like this are used to test animal intelligence, to see if an animal recognizes the reflection as itself or thinks it is another animal.

# CAUGHT RED-HANDED

JEFF
Geobiologist

## DESCRIBE YOUR SOLUTION.

I keep my candy stash in a drawer of my desk, so I would put some double-sided tape on the handle of the drawer. When the thief touches the drawer, fingerprints would be captured on the tape. Then I would compare the prints with those of my top suspects! All I need is some double-sided tape and a fingerprinting kit.

## WHAT WERE YOUR FIRST THOUGHTS WHEN YOU READ THE CHALLENGE?

At first, my goal was to stop the thief from taking my candy. This would protect my stash, but the thief might go steal someone else's candy. So it seemed like finding a way to actually identify the thief, rather than just stop the theft, would be better for everyone!

## WHAT OTHER SOLUTIONS DID YOU CONSIDER?

One idea was to trap the thief in my room by using string to connect the door handle to the desk drawer, triggering the door to shut and lock when the desk was opened. I also considered putting a tracking device on the candy bar wrapper, but that would be expensive and would only work if the thief carried the candy around with him or her.

More Solutions

THE NAT GEO ENGINEERS REALLY GOT INTO THIS ONE. THEY CAME UP WITH A SWEET—BUT COMPLICATED— SOLUTION.

Challenge #2: Protect Your Candy Stash

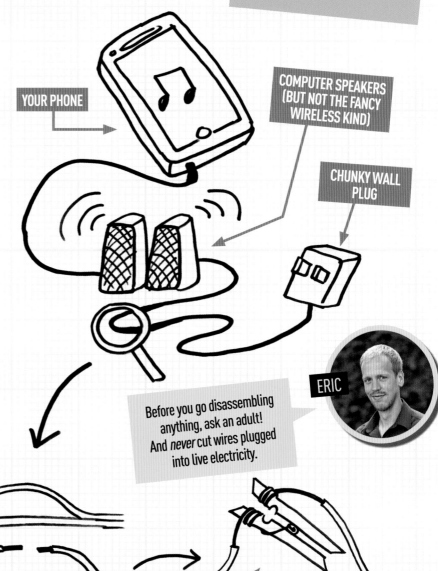

YOUR PHONE

COMPUTER SPEAKERS (BUT NOT THE FANCY WIRELESS KIND)

CHUNKY WALL PLUG

What you need is a chunky wall plug from your computer speakers. It takes your wall power and converts it down to a lower voltage so you don't electrocute yourself or your little brother.

MIKE

You need something to interrupt the power. All you have to do is interrupt one of the wires by cutting it. That's what gets connected to the switch.

ERIC

Before you go disassembling anything, ask an adult! And never cut wires plugged into live electricity.

You need to expose a bunch of copper wire so you can wrap it around your clothespin.

ATTACH EACH SIDE OF THE CUT WIRE TO A SIDE OF THE CLOTHESPIN. THE WIRE SHOULD TOUCH WHEN THE CLOTHESPIN IS CLOSED.

CONNECT A PLASTIC CARD, LIKE AN OLD GIFT CARD, TO A STRING, AND ATTACH THAT STRING TO THE CANDY STASH!

This is pretty fun. We should just do these kinds of challenges all the time instead of our real jobs ...

ERIC

PLACE THE CARD INSIDE THE CLOTHESPIN. GET YOUR FAVORITE PLAYLIST STARTED ON YOUR PHONE (BUT DON'T EXPECT TO HEAR ANY MUSIC YET).

MIKE

You'll want to tie the clothespin to something sturdy nearby so your little sibling doesn't pull everything with the candy bowl.

WHEN THE ROBBER COMES FOR YOUR STASH, THE CARD WILL COME OUT OF THE CLOTHESPIN. THE WIRES WILL TOUCH, AND THE MUSIC WILL START TO PLAY. YOU HAVE YOUR VERY OWN CANDY STASH ALARM SYSTEM.

TOM

To make it look less suspicious, try to cover up your string with clothes or trash.

# THE CHALLENGE

## ITTY-BITTY BIKE RAMP

**OBJECTIVE:** CREATE A SCALE MODEL TO WORK ON YOUR BIKE MOVES

### The Situation

You want to practice getting some air, but the nearest bike park is too far away. You decide to build a scale model "bike course" to plan your moves. How can you model your moves in the backyard using a playground ball as a stand-in for yourself? (Hey, you don't want to get hurt!)

# SOLUTIONS

Challenge #3: Create a Scale Model to Work on Your Bike Moves

## POWER PLAY

RYAN
Coral Reef Biologist

### DESCRIBE YOUR SOLUTION.

First, I would toss the ball down the inclined roof of a doghouse, which would send it to a small plastic toddler-size slide (the kind with a bend in it). The ball would turn sharply and bounce off a small trampoline at the end, thanks to the elasticity of the springs. I would then catch the ball and try the loop again, making adjustments to get the best speed and most air. (Sweet moves, right?)

### WHAT WERE YOUR FIRST THOUGHTS WHEN YOU READ THE CHALLENGE?

My first thoughts were about choosing materials that would be found in a typical home or backyard. I wondered how I could get the ball up to speed without building any structures that would take up more space in the backyard. What would it take for the ball to make sharp turns and get up to speed with a minimal amount of effort?

### WHAT OTHER SOLUTIONS DID YOU CONSIDER?

I also considered making some sort of slingshot to get up to speed. Another idea was to take advantage of the same kind of elasticity that is present in trampoline springs, but with other materials. I decided these plans were too complicated since they involved items I might not be able to find in the backyard. My first idea was to simply allow the ball to roll down the side of a doghouse and bounce off the fence and back to me. I rejected this plan because the ball would not reach enough speed to rebound from the fence. This is why I chose to add the curving slide and trampoline. I knew these objects would close the final distance and bring the ball closer to me.

**CINDY**
*Geologist*

## WHAT WAS YOUR FIRST IDEA? WAS IT YOUR BEST ONE?

When making a model, it's important to think about how to mimic full-size forces at a smaller size. I wondered whether I could create more distance for increasing speed by using two ramps, opposite each other. This would (a) prevent energy from being lost around tight curves, (b) increase the distance leading up to the second ramp, and (c) make it possible to take advantage of potential energy to go faster, as gravity increases speed down the first ramp. This was my best and first idea.

## WHAT WERE YOUR CRITERIA FOR A SUCCESSFUL SOLUTION?

The solution satisfies the criteria of needing to increase distance without creating a track with tight curves. It is a successful solution if the two bike ramps allow you to increase the distance you travel between the starting point and the second ramp's entrance, and you go faster as a result. I think the main test of this solution would be through trial and error.

# SEESAW SOLUTION

When making up this scenario, I thought the Explorers might suggest a series of steep wooden ramps or ideas on how to experiment using playground balls of various sizes.

The goal for building a model is to find ways to keep momentum going in a smaller space. My solution is to dig into the ground to hollow out a dip on the "bike" path and then use the soil to build up a hill. I would position a seesaw on the downward-side slope of the dip, then rapidly roll a ball into the dip. Traveling down the slope would cause the ball to build up enough speed to travel over the hill and reach the seesaw. Just as it rolled to the far side, I'd slam the opposite end down to propel the ball into the air.

Once I got all the forces and angles right for the ramp, I would build devices for the rest of the course, one by one. Then I could rearrange the model's components to ensure the best sequence to maximize energy from one feature to the next.

**JOAN**
*Author*

More Solutions

# SOLUTIONS

THE NAT GEO ENGINEERS HAD A *RUFF* IDEA OF HOW TO APPROACH THIS CHALLENGE!

Challenge #3: Create a Scale Model to Work on Your Bike Moves

 a ball

 rocks

 cardboard

FIND STUFF AROUND THE HOUSE TO HELP YOU BUILD.

Since you don't have much room, build a ramp to increase your potential energy and let gravity increase your speed.

BRAD

If you were building a human-size ramp, you'd probably want to build one that starts as high as the roof of your house. But we're building a scale model! And what's a scale model of your house? Your dog's house!

TOM

# THE CHALLENGE

## SPECIAL DELIVERY

### OBJECTIVE: TRANSPORT AN OBJECT BETWEEN TWO WINDOWS

## The Situation

Your friend left a library book at your house, but you can't return it because you're quarantined with the flu. Fortunately, you live next door to one another and your bedroom windows are across a mere 15-foot (5-m) expanse. How can you deliver the goods without leaving your room?

DOES YOUR FRIEND NEED THE ACTUAL BOOK OR JUST SOME PAGES? DEFINING THE PROBLEM WILL HELP WITH DESIGNING THE SOLUTION!

# NUMBER 4

WHEELS AND AXLES COULD BE USEFUL!

SOLUTIONS!

Challenge #4: Transport an Object Between Two Windows

## >> SMOOTH SAILING

### ERIKA
Deep-Sea Submersible Pilot

**DESCRIBE YOUR SOLUTION.**
First we need to get our transport line between the two windows, but the rope I have is too heavy to throw. The smaller diameter rope that I can throw will be too light and won't make it the distance to the other window. To solve this, I make a heavy knot called a "monkey's fist" on the end of a light rope and attach it to a heavier rope using a sheepshank knot. We use the monkey's fist to throw the rope back and forth between the windows, and we each loop the rope around a table leg. Now one big loop of rope connects our rooms. As I pull on the top rope, the loop will travel between the rooms. I attach a bucket to the rope with another piece of rope, then we pull on the main rope to pass the book. And voilà! Thanks to my sailor knots, it's reading time!

**WHAT WERE YOUR FIRST THOUGHTS WHEN YOU READ THE CHALLENGE?**
This is just like what we used to do on the ship when we wanted to pass things between bunks in the forecastle; I'm going to need to get really good at tying knots! Right away, I knew that I wanted to create a pulley system for the rope. What I couldn't immediately decide was whether I actually needed pulleys and how I would get one over to my friend. I wondered if the entire system might be low enough in friction to make it possible to tow the rope without pulleys.

**WHAT OTHER SOLUTIONS DID YOU CONSIDER?**
Sending the rope over was the biggest challenge. I thought of throwing something heavy like a rock with the rope tied around it but realized I might hit a window and break something. That would be bad news, so I put the kibosh on that. Simplicity in engineering was important to me.

## KEEP IT SIMPLE

**DENISE**
Archaeologist

### DESCRIBE YOUR SOLUTION.

The simplest thing seems to be to open the window just a crack and pass the book over to the boy outside, assuming he is the friend we're talking about. Or, if he is not, ask him to give it to the intended friend in the other window. I'd be sure to wash my hands and put on some gloves and a face mask before opening the window and handing over the book, just to be on the safe side and avoid passing around my infection.

### WHY DID YOU CHOOSE THESE SPECIFIC MATERIALS AND TOOLS?

The face mask and gloves provided a simple way to keep my germs to myself. I chose a human agent as my tool because it was the quickest, most direct method to solving the problem. Using other materials would have overcomplicated my solution.

### HOW COULD YOUR SOLUTION BE USED FOR A REAL-WORLD PROBLEM?

For this answer, I remember a joke I heard a long time ago. It said something like the following: "Some astronauts needed to write things down in space. One space agency developed a very expensive pen that could write in zero gravity, upside down, and stand very high pressures and temperatures. Another space agency gave their astronauts pencils." I think that engineering solutions using machinery and tools are very important and always an excellent option, but when we have real-world problems, it's also essential that we don't get carried away with technology and that we remember that simple, straightforward solutions can also be just what we need.

## SHARP SHOOTER

**CONSTANCE**
Space Architect

### DESCRIBE YOUR SOLUTION.

Attach a 30-foot (9-m) rope to an arrow with a suction-cup end. Fire the arrow from your bedroom to your friend's. The friend would need to have the window open and stand well out of range to avoid possible injury. Once my friend has the rope in hand, tie the book to the end of the rope so she can pull it across.

### WHAT WAS YOUR FIRST IDEA? WAS IT YOUR BEST ONE?

I considered trying to throw the book between the windows but realized it would probably fall short. The book would flop open as it sailed through the air.

### WHAT WERE YOUR CRITERIA FOR A SUCCESSFUL SOLUTION?

She gets her book, of course! Plus, neither my friend nor her house gets hurt.

More Solutions

# NAT GEO ENGINEER SOLUTIONS

**Challenge #4:** Transport an Object Between Two Windows

BRAD

TAKE PICTURES OF THE BOOK PAGES AND EMAIL THEM TO YOUR FRIEND.

If your bud just wants to read and doesn't need the physical book, you could take pictures with your phone or scan the book and send the pages by email. This seems uncomplicated, but it is by far the most complicated ...

Other people have created technology to solve all kinds of real problems; you just add your own ingenuity to it.

... because the email has to go up into space and back down to reach your friend.

TOM

ERIC

Now, if your bud needs the physical book, we'll need to get creative.

BRAD

**TIE SHEETS TOGETHER TO MAKE ROPE.**

①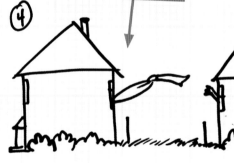

②

**PROTECT THE BOOK IN A PILLOWCASE OR BOOK BAG.**

Ask your friend to set up a bunch of pillows to protect the bedroom walls. Put the book in a pillowcase, tape it shut, tell your friend to step aside, and throw it as hard as you can through the window.

③

**TIE THE ROPE TO THE PILLOWCASE THAT CONTAINS THE BOOK.**

**TOSS THE END OF THE SHEET TO YOUR FRIEND.**

④

⑤

MIKE

**TELL YOUR FRIEND TO REEL IN THE SHEET TO GET THE BOOK.**

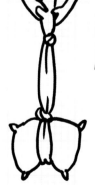

# THE CHALLENGE

## STOLEN STUFFY

**OBJECTIVE:** CROSS THE CREEK TO RETRIEVE THE STUFFED ANIMAL

### The Situation

You're hanging out outside, when a golden eagle thinks your little sister's best stuffy is a dead squirrel. It swoops down and carries it away before realizing fake fur isn't delicious. The eagle drops the toy on the other side of a creek, and now your sister's crying so loud you think your head is going to explode. How can you cross the creek quickly to retrieve the toy without getting wet?

TOO BAD YOUR ARMS AREN'T LONG ENOUGH TO JUST REACH ACROSS ... HINT, HINT.

NO HOUSEHOLD ITEMS HERE. YOU'LL REALLY HAVE TO GET CREATIVE!

SOLUTIONS!

# SOLUTIONS

Challenge #5: Cross the Creek to Retrieve the Stuffed Animal

>> STICKY SITUATION

### RYAN
Coral Reef Biologist

### DESCRIBE YOUR SOLUTION.

My solution allows me to retrieve the stuffy without putting myself in danger or becoming completely soaked! I would take a rope (or make a rope out of vines or clothes if necessary) and tie a rock onto the end to provide the weight needed to throw it across the creek. Next I would cover the rock with a material that would stick to the stuffy—tape or a strip of the hooked side of the closure from my backpack pockets or shoe strap, held on with elastics or tape. When the rock sailed over the water and struck the stuffy, it would stick, allowing me to pull it back without getting my clothes wet!

### WHAT WAS YOUR FIRST IDEA? WAS IT YOUR BEST ONE?

My first idea was to use fallen logs or other items, like car tires, to make a stepping bridge across the creek. I don't think this was my best idea as it would take much longer than my plan to swing a rope across the creek and I have to make my sister's crying stop! As well, if the creek is quite deep or too fast flowing, my bridge would simply fall apart during construction. It would also be difficult to test any of my bridge design ideas on the land or expect them to work in the water on the first try. Plus, it would be too dangerous.

### WHAT WERE YOUR CRITERIA FOR A SUCCESSFUL SOLUTION?

My success criteria were:

1) All of the items used were either nearby or easy to make.
2) Practice tests worked. Testing would involve using a piece of fabric similar to the plush and putting it the same distance away from me on land. I would test the tool multiple times to ensure I could pull the object back from the same distance each time.
3) The stuffy was brought back across the creek, with no parts of the tool left behind.
4) From start to finish, the rescue was completed very quickly.
5) My sister stopped crying.

## >> GONE FISHIN'

JEFF
Geobiologist

### DESCRIBE YOUR SOLUTION.

To retrieve the stuffed animal, I would use a fishing pole as a grappling hook! It's pretty similar to the eagle's talons, actually. By casting the line across the creek and getting the fishhook into the stuffed animal, I could then reel it back in to our side of the rapids. This might take several tries, but I would probably develop some good fishing skills! On the other hand, I'd ask my parents to cast the line instead. They're probably better at hitting a fishing target, anyway!

### WHY DID YOU CHOOSE THESE SPECIFIC MATERIALS AND TOOLS?

A fishing pole is simple to operate. Everything needed to get the hook across the water is in one tool. Using a fishing pole instead of crossing the creek minimizes risk. Repurposing common household items, instead of building something new, is an important part of this solution.

### HOW COULD YOUR SOLUTION BE USED FOR A REAL-WORLD PROBLEM?

The challenge of moving large objects (like people and the systems needed to support them) is something NASA scientists and engineers think about when designing space missions. Humans need food, water, and air, so transporting them across the solar system to other planets like Mars takes a really big, expensive rocket. Sending robots instead, like the Curiosity Mars rover, makes things less complicated and cheaper. We're using the same idea here to keep my sister and me out of harm's way!

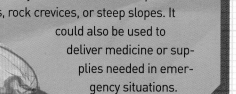

## >> HOOK, LINE, AND STUFFY

CECELIA
Archaeologist

### DESCRIBE YOUR SOLUTION.

Instead of trying any risky solution, I would try to "catch" the stuffed bear using a fishing rod. If the surface of the bear turns out to be too hard to hook, I would attach the insect net to the end of the fishing rod, then try to scoop the bear.

### WHY DID YOU CHOOSE THESE SPECIFIC MATERIALS AND TOOLS?

I chose a fishing rod because it's a tool that is designed to catch things from a certain distance. It has a nonslip handle that is easy to grip, a hook to snag the object, and string to help with retrieval. Also, it is very easy to use.

### HOW COULD YOUR SOLUTION BE USED FOR A REAL-WORLD PROBLEM?

This solution could be applied in real-life situations to recover objects in hard-to-reach places such as wells, rock crevices, or steep slopes. It could also be used to deliver medicine or supplies needed in emergency situations.

More Solutions

# SOLUTIONS

THE NAT GEO ENGINEERS BECAME STUFFY SUPERHEROES WITH THESE DETAILED RESCUE MISSION PLANS.

**Challenge #5:** Cross the Creek to Retrieve the Stuffed Animal

MAKE THE TARP INTO A PARACHUTE SCOOP.

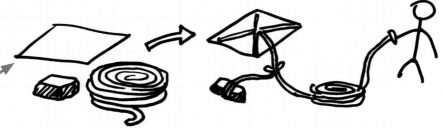

Take a rope and some tarp to make a small parachute-like shape with four corners, then tie a rock to one of the corners so it's heavy enough to throw. Hold one end of the rope and throw it across to capture the stuffy. Reel it back using the rope.

TOM

Or you could use duct tape or string to lash several sticks together to make a pole. Put a big wad of chewed bubble gum on the end or make a hook using sticks or nails. Try to snag the stuffy and pull it back.

# THE CHALLENGE

## SOUR SELL-OFF

### OBJECTIVE: CREATE A SCALE TO WEIGH CANDY

## The Situation

Your favorite bulk candy store was having a major sale. You lost control and came home with 10 pounds (5 kg) of sour candies. After recovering from a sudden stomachache, you decide to go into business and sell your leftovers in half-pound (.25-kg) portions. How can you measure the correct weights without buying a scale?

NUMBER 6

THE CANDY IS ALL DIFFERENT SIZES AND SHAPES ... THAT COULD MAKE THINGS DIFFICULT.

10 LBS

HOW CAN KNOWING THE WEIGHT OF ONE OBJECT HELP YOU FIND THE WEIGHT OF A DIFFERENT OBJECT?

SOLUTIONS!

# SOLUTIONS

Challenge #6: Create a Scale to Weigh Candy

ERIKA
Deep-Sea
Submersible Pilot

## >> A MEASURED RESPONSE

**DESCRIBE YOUR SOLUTION.**
I constructed a scale by balancing a ruler on a ball bearing. The ball is seated in an eggcup with a slightly smaller diameter. Grooves cut into the eggcup match the ruler's width, allowing the ruler to rock without sliding off the ball bearing. I attach two identical plates to both ends of the ruler with clay. Voilà! A balance scale. Now I need a reference object. I place a one-pound (0.5-kg) hand weight on one scale and pile sand from the yard onto the other plate until both sides are balanced. Pouring the pound of sand into a measuring cup shows me its volume. Dumping out half the volume leaves me with half the weight—half a pound (.25 kg). Now I remove the one-pound weight, replace it with my half pound of sand, and I have a reference weight to measure my candy into portions.

**WHY DID YOU CHOOSE THESE SPECIFIC MATERIALS AND TOOLS?**
Using a ruler for the lever arm between the two objects to be balanced meant I didn't have to do any work to figure out the perfect fulcrum for the scale. I simply used the ruler's measurement marks to find the exact center.

**HOW COULD YOUR SOLUTION BE USED FOR A REAL-WORLD PROBLEM?**
When you hold two objects, you can often tell (to several grams) which object is heavier. However, a balance scale is needed for higher precision, such as when you need to weigh and measure products for sale such as fish, gold, or candy!

## SWEET DIVISION

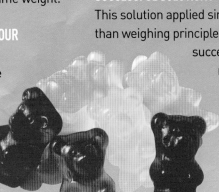

**DESCRIBE YOUR SOLUTION.**

Don't weigh it—portion it! Dividing 10 pounds (5 kg) of candy into 0.5-pound (.25-kg) portions would create 20 equal portions. I would make 20 equal piles of candy by doling out one candy at a time per pile. Each pile would have the same number of candies in it and should equal the same weight.

**WHAT WAS YOUR FIRST IDEA? WAS IT YOUR BEST ONE?**

My first and best solution was to use math to predict weight by creating the equal portions instead of figuring out how to weigh it. Of course, that assumes that all of the candy in the bag is the same size and weight. If it's different sizes, it would be much harder to predict the weight of each.

**WHAT WERE YOUR CRITERIA FOR A SUCCESSFUL SOLUTION?**

This solution applied simple mathematics rather than weighing principles. My revised criterion for success was to eliminate the need for weighing by accurately separating the candy into 20 equal half-pound portions. No materials were harmed in this challenge.

**CINDY**
*Geologist*

## FLOUR POWER

**RYAN**
*Coral Reef Biologist*

**DESCRIBE YOUR SOLUTION.**

My solution would be to find an item in the house, such as a bag of flour, that weighs the same as the desired candy portion. I would then make a balance using a piece of wood set across a triangular fulcrum. After placing the flour on one side of the scale, I would add candies to the other side until both sides were balanced.

**WHY DID YOU CHOOSE THESE SPECIFIC MATERIALS AND TOOLS?**

I considered whether my choices would be sturdy enough to hold a half-pound of weight on each side of the balance long enough for all of the candy to be weighed.

**HOW COULD YOUR SOLUTION BE USED FOR A REAL-WORLD PROBLEM?**

My solution could be used to measure scientific samples in the field, such as the tropical rain forest, where it might be difficult to access an accurate scale due to the moist environment or an absence of electricity. One of the benefits of this solution is its portability. The simple materials it requires would be light and easy to carry on any expedition.

More Solutions

# SOLUTIONS

THE NAT GEO ENGINEERS GOT MATHEMATICAL WITH THEIR CANDY-COUNTING SOLUTIONS.

**Challenge #6:** Create a Scale to Weigh Candy

① **FIND THE TOTAL WEIGHT.**

Find out how much each candy weighs by counting how many you have and dividing the number of pieces into the total weight. That should give you the average weight per piece. Then count the pieces to make equal portions.

BRAD

② **COUNT THE NUMBER OF PIECES.**

③ **FIND THE AVERAGE WEIGHT PER PIECE.**

④ **DIVIDE THE CANDY INTO EQUAL PORTIONS.**

$$= \text{weight} \div \text{\# of pieces}$$

You should definitely do that, but what if the buyer doesn't believe the amount is right? You could show the portion size by making a balance. Start by finding 10 pounds of something else that you could divide up easily.

You could use pennies.

ERIC

TOM

76

= 1/2 lb of
pennies
(or some coin)

ERIC

SOUR CANDIES

MAKE EQUAL PORTIONS BY BALANCING THE SCALE.

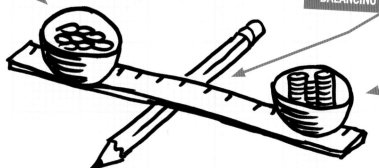

PENNIES

measure candy
out so it balances
against a standard
of 1/2 lb of coins
(or something else that
weighs 1/2 lb)

TOM

MAKE A BALANCE WITH HOUSEHOLD ITEMS: A RULER, CUPS, AND A PENCIL.

Knowing for sure how much one side weighs will help you know how much the other side weighs.

# THE CHALLENGE

## DON'T LET THE BEDBUGS BITE

**OBJECTIVE:** BUILD A HAMMOCK TO AVOID BEDBUGS

### The Situation

Bedbugs invaded your house, so you're sleeping under the stars tonight. Not wanting to be in the tent with your smelly siblings and dragon-breath dog, you decide a hammock will do just fine. There's only one problem. No one is willing to cough up the dough for your own private bedroom between the trees. You decide to make a hammock with materials from outside the house. How can you do it without using any material that might be infected with bedbugs?

WHO NEEDS WALLS WHEN YOU'VE GOT TREES, RIGHT?

YOUR BEDSHEET ISN'T THE ONLY COMFY CLOTH AROUND.

SOLUTIONS!

# SOLUTIONS

## Challenge #7: Build a Hammock to Avoid Bedbugs

>> MOSSY MATTRESS

**RYAN**
*Coral Reef Biologist*

### WHAT WAS YOUR FIRST IDEA? WAS IT YOUR BEST ONE?

My first idea was to hang a sleeping bag like a cocoon from the trees in the back-yard for a comfortable night's sleep. This was not my best idea as it wouldn't be a "true" hammock, nor would it give me a relaxing night with a perfect view of the stars. I would have to poke my head out to see anything! I also considered making a hammock out of a long wooden toboggan, secured at each end by trees. After some thought, I decided to reject this solution. The boards would be incredibly uncomfortable and the sled would be difficult and heavy to hang from the trees without help from other family members.

In the end, my solution was to build a hammock using materials from the garage—a standard blue tarp and nylon rope. To make it a more comfy place to sleep, I would collect a large number of ferns, mosses, and other non-prickly plants and cover myself with the plants for insulation. If it turned out to be difficult to find enough plants, I would supplement the cushioning material with sponges from the garage and the life jackets lying around the backyard. If I could find an uninfected sleeping bag in the attic of the garage, I would definitely choose it first for making a snug bed under the stars!

### WHAT WERE YOUR CRITERIA FOR A SUCCESSFUL SOLUTION?

Testing my hammock for bedbugs would involve examining it very closely with a microscope or magnifying glass. I would test the hammock's ability to hold my weight by filling it with heavy objects, of approximately the same weight as myself, and leaving them there for several hours prior to bed-time. This would tell me whether stronger materials, or other adjustments, were required.

The criteria for a successful solution are:

1) The hammock could be created cheaply from easy-to-access materials.

2) I would wake up in the morning without any bedbug bites.

3) I would be comfortable enough to stay in my hammock the entire night.

4) The design would allow me to watch the stars as I slowly fell asleep.

# SNUG—BUT NO BUGS!

**ERIKA**
Deep-Sea
Submersible Pilot

### DESCRIBE YOUR SOLUTION.

So simple. Grab a big sleeping bag and two long pieces of rope. Tie a clove hitch to each end of the bag and use the same knot to attach the other end of the ropes to two trees. The clove hitch will ensure my weight locks the knots down tighter instead of pulling them out. To protect the trees from friction, slip cardboard between the rope and the bark. Unzip the sleeping bag and climb into a cozy, hanging cocoon.

### WHY DID YOU CHOOSE THESE SPECIFIC MATERIALS AND TOOLS?

Using a sleeping bag rather than a simple sheet ensures that the airflow at night is buffered and I'll stay warmer. The shape is also ideal because I can zip myself in and keep the mosquitoes off.

### HOW COULD YOUR SOLUTION BE USED FOR A REAL-WORLD PROBLEM?

Mosquitoes transmit malaria and other diseases in many parts of the world. People can help protect themselves by tying a mosquito net structure between trees, using the same knot and tie-down method used to build a hammock.

---

# BADMINTON BEDDING

**MUNAZZA**
Astronomer

### DESCRIBE YOUR SOLUTION.

The badminton net in the backyard will serve as my makeshift hammock! It's stretchy and flexible. I'd drape the picnic blanket on top to have a more stable material to sleep on (one without mesh holes!), and I'd use thick rope and strong parents to mount the hammock between the trees.

### WHAT WAS YOUR FIRST IDEA? WAS IT YOUR BEST ONE?

My first idea included constructing a hammock from thick blankets, but that wasn't a good solution considering that they might be infected with bedbugs. It's great to brainstorm while thinking of solutions, especially since combinations of ideas can be great solutions!

### WHAT WERE YOUR CRITERIA FOR A SUCCESSFUL SOLUTION?

My criteria were to create a practical, comfortable, and bedbug-free hammock. To succeed, I'd need to use something from the backyard or the garage that is stretchy, soft, and capable of being tied/mounted to the trees.

More Solutions

# NAT GEO ENGINEER SOLUTIONS

**Challenge #7:** Build a Hammock to Avoid Bedbugs

LAYER UP A COUPLE OF SHEETS AND TIE A CLOTHESLINE TIGHTLY TO THE END FOR A BURRITO-STYLE HAMMOCK THAT WRAPS AROUND YOU WHEN YOU SLEEP.

Your parents are probably strong, so ask them to tie your knots!

TOM

DON'T TIE YOUR HAMMOCK TOO FAR FROM THE GROUND—JUST IN CASE!

If you want a deluxe, non-burrito hammock, attach the sheets to boards or broom handles.

MIKE

# THE CHALLENGE

## DESERT DRINK

### OBJECTIVE: CREATE A SOURCE OF DRINKING WATER

### The Situation

You're hiking through the desert looking for semiprecious stones when sunlight glints off the ground. Could it be the obsidian you've been searching for? You drop to your knees for a closer look, unaware you've caused your water bottle to tip. By the time you realize you've only spotted a bit of worn glass, your water bottle has drained into the sand. How are you going to get more water without leaving the desert?

NATURE CAN BE GREAT INSPIRATION!

THINK FAST! YOUR WATER IS EVAPORATING IN THE HOT SUN ...

SOLUTIONS!

# SOLUTIONS

Challenge #8: Create a Source of Drinking Water

## >> SPEEDY RECOVERY

CINDY
Geologist

### DESCRIBE YOUR SOLUTION.

Harness the power of evaporation! Scoop the wet sand back into your water bottle quickly, and put the cap on the bottle. As the bottle warms up in the daytime sun, the water stuck in the damp sand will evaporate. As the air in the top of the bottle cools down (perhaps when night falls), the water vapor in the air space in the top of the bottle will condense into droplets. You can pour off those water droplets and drink them. Repeat as long as water condenses on the top of the bottle, or until you run out of damp sand.

### WHY DID YOU CHOOSE THIS STRATEGY?

It seemed like the most reasonable use of the natural environment. I often carry a plastic bottle of water with

me throughout the day, and many times I leave a half-full bottle of water in my car overnight. When I come out the next morning (after a cool night), there are often droplets of water condensed at the top of the bottle. Seeing this every day makes me think that if you could just create a similar phenomenon (with hot ambient air temperature that then cools down), you could retrieve the water from the sand.

### HOW COULD YOUR SOLUTION OR RESULTS BE APPLIED TO REAL-WORLD PROBLEMS?

Beetles and other critters do this in deserts, so it makes sense. Beetles in the Namib Desert (which is on the west coast of Africa) hang upside down throughout the night so that any dew that condenses on them runs down toward (and eventually into) their mouths. It's a great way to "make" water in a desert. You could do the same thing on a larger scale (try to collect condensing water vapor) in arid regions.

**DENISE**
Archaeologist

### DESCRIBE YOUR SOLUTION.

I'm aware that cacti hold water reserves within them. My solution involves identifying a species of cactus that contains water that is safe for drinking. Not all cacti contain safe water! After finding a safe cactus, I gather the tools I had carefully selected before leaving home and stored in my dog's pack. This includes antibacterial gel and tissues, which I use to clean the glass I found. I make a small but deep hole on the side of the trunk, and use the glass to make a tap. (If I didn't have a knife, I could use the glass to make the hole.) By lifting the tap, I can collect drips of water into my bottle.

### WHY DID YOU CHOOSE THESE SPECIFIC MATERIALS AND TOOLS?

It's important to be prepared for emergencies when you pack a bag to go out into the field. It was reassuring to know that I had some basic tools and first-aid supplies with me. When I thought of the way sap is harvested from trees to make maple syrup, I got the idea to try to harvest water.

### HOW COULD YOUR SOLUTION BE USED FOR A REAL-WORLD PROBLEM?

In the real world, before you head out to any potentially dangerous areas, it's good to think about what you would do in an emergency. Talking to a cactus expert to learn what kinds of cacti are safe to drink could save your life in the desert.

**JOAN**
Author

I'd collect condensation using a clear plastic bag, one of my shoelaces, and a leafy branch. The branch has to be strong enough to hold the water's weight and the plant must not be poisonous or have waxy leaves. I place the bag around the leafiest branch I can find, trying to keep it full of air, like a balloon. One corner should hang lower than the other to collect the water. Holding the bag closed, I tie my shoelace as tightly as possible to seal it shut. It is important to stop air from flowing out, so the bag cannot have any holes.

My solution takes advantage of the fact that water exits plants through their leaves in a process called transpiration. As sunlight shines on the bag, water escaping the leaves will collect in the bottom of the bag instead of evaporating. The plastic bag, which holds warm air around the leaves, will cause the leaves to transpire more quickly. If I have more bags and more shoelaces, I can collect even more water.

More Solutions

# NAT GEO ENGINEER SOLUTIONS

THE NAT GEO ENGINEERS REALLY DUG THEMSELVES DEEP INTO THIS ONE. AND THEY FOUND A WAY TO RECYCLE TRASH IN THE PROCESS!

**Challenge #8:** Create a Source of Drinking Water

DIG A HOLE.

PUT THE WET SAND AT THE BOTTOM.

You'll need to find a plastic bag.

ERIC

PLACE YOUR BOTTLE OR A BUCKET HERE.

That should be easy because there are plastic bags all over the desert. Recycle and reuse!

The water will evaporate and condense on the sides of the bag.

MIKE

ERIC

88

## ROMANTIC RESCUE

### OBJECTIVE: MAKE A BACKYARD WATERFALL

### The Situation

Your big brother is freaking out. He's invited his girlfriend over for a romantic picnic by the backyard waterfall, but the tiny creek that flows into it is dry. The lovesick puppy promises to teach you his trick basketball shot if you figure out a way to get the water flowing again—at least for an hour. After you agree, he mentions that you can't use the garden hose because your parents took it to the cabin. How can you create some watery backyard magic?

YOUR BIKE MIGHT BE HELPFUL FOR SOMETHING OTHER THAN ESCAPING ONCE THE SMOOCHING STARTS!

HMM ... LOOKS LIKE THE FAMILY DOG MIGHT BE ONTO SOMETHING ...

SOLUTIONS!

# SOLUTIONS

### Challenge #9: Make a Backyard Waterfall

RYAN
*Coral Reef Biologist*

>> **UNDER PRESSURE**

### DESCRIBE YOUR SOLUTION.

My solution to maintain the waterfall is to use a regular garden shovel to dig a small trench in the ground, similar to an irrigation ditch. The water would travel from the backyard faucet (which would still be there, attached to the house, even if your parents took the hose) to the creek. During testing, I found the water pressure at the source so intense, it blasted the dirt out of the ground and created a deep hole. To prevent erosion, I placed a piece of wood on the ground where the water exited the faucet. This dissipated the energy of the pressurized water and stopped the water from getting dirty.

Using a trench to transport water is an ancient solution—in fact, I modeled my method on current and past irrigation canals and ditches designed to bring water to dry areas.

### WHAT WAS YOUR FIRST IDEA? WAS IT YOUR BEST ONE?

My first idea was to fold a plastic tarp in half to form a type of "slide" to transfer the water to the creek and waterfall. This was not my best idea.

Water running along the plastic would probably be quite noisy. It would be difficult to suspend multiple tarps, and they would present an eyesore that would impact the experience of the picnic! I also considered filling a rain barrel with water and moving it to the head of the creek or waterfall. Removing a plug would create a slow and steady stream of water for the duration of the pic-nic. I rejected this plan because it would take more than a barrel full of water to make a beautiful waterfall for the length of a picnic.

### WHAT WERE YOUR CRITERIA FOR A SUCCESSFUL SOLUTION?

1) The volume of water reaching the dry creek bed would allow the waterfall to flow during the entire picnic.
2) The materials that made the waterfall possible would not be noticeable or create an eyesore.
3) The design would offer a relatively quiet solution.

## CATCH & RELEASE

JEFF
Geobiologist

### DESCRIBE YOUR SOLUTION.

This one will require careful planning and a serious workout! I don't want to permanently change the creek's ecosystem, as plants and animals have adapted to live in the stream in its natural state. To get the waterfall going again, I would dam the creek upstream using rocks, sticks, leaves, and mud to create a large, temporary pool of water. When the time comes, I can release the water and the waterfall will be restored.

### WHY DID YOU CHOOSE THESE SPECIFIC MATERIALS AND TOOLS?

Even though we'll need a lot of material to make a dam large enough for our needs, rocks, sticks, mud, sand, and leaves are readily available. Tools to move these materials, like shovels or buckets, are simple, common household objects. It's a low-tech solution.

### HOW COULD YOUR SOLUTION BE USED FOR A REAL-WORLD PROBLEM?

Containing and shifting fluids is useful for flood control and crop irrigation. Reservoirs can be created to provide a reliable source of water to farms; generate a consistent, safe flow of river water; and make energy. These can be very useful benefits to society, but it's important to think about how big changes to the flow of the river could modify and potentially harm native plants and animals.

---

## PEDAL PUSHER

ERIKA
Deep-Sea Submersible Pilot

### WHAT WAS YOUR FIRST IDEA? WAS IT YOUR BEST ONE?

I considered making a water pump using a bike on a pedal stand. A shaft on the rear hub would connect to a sealed bucket of water with an inlet and outlet. Peddling would build up pressure to pump water to the top of the waterfall. It was a good idea because it wouldn't waste tons of water but not the best idea because I couldn't make it without a garden hose.

### WHAT WERE YOUR CRITERIA FOR A SUCCESSFUL SOLUTION?

I chose to shoot water into the creek by using plumbing to create a high-pressure laminar flow stream—one that is constant and uninterrupted, like you see in a fountain. Success depended on the nozzle's ability to shoot water far enough. It had to be correctly aligned to prevent the water from encountering rough edges and spraying haphazardly. There could be no leaks, which would reduce water pressure.

More Solutions

# NAT GEO ENGINEER
# SOLUTIONS

## Challenge #9: Make a Backyard Waterfall

USE DIRT FROM THE HOLE TO FORM A DAM.

① 

② 

RESERVOIR

TOM

You can make a reservoir at the top of the waterfall. Your big brother is probably stronger, so get him to dig a pit at the top of the waterfall. Line it with a tarp and get him to carry the water. You can open the dam at the right moment.

This is a lot of work. I hope he's going to marry this girl.

BRAD

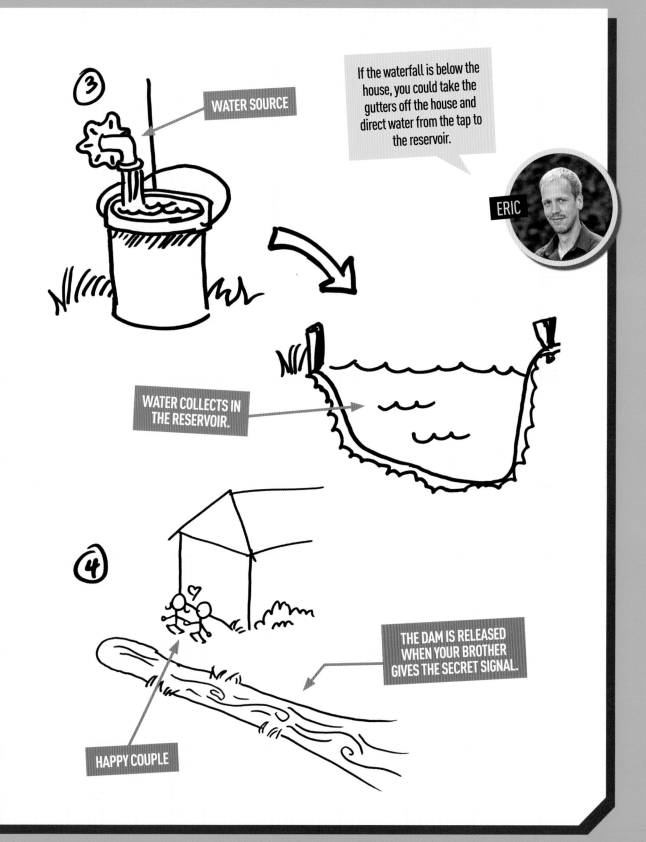

# THE CHALLENGE

## SCURVY SKEETERS

**OBJECTIVE: CREATE CLOTHING TO PROTECT YOU FROM MOSQUITOES**

## The Situation

Your friends are coming over to celebrate the most important day of the year—Pirate Parrrrrty Day. As you adjust your hook arm, a loud humming draws you to the window. A whole bunch of mosquitoes are swarming around the house. That's bad news for guests trying to reach the front door. You decide to move your party to the end of the driveway, but the only way out there is through the bitey bunch. What kind of protective clothing can you create that will save you from the mosquitoes but still fit with your pirate theme?

PIRATE PROPS PROVIDE PLENTIFUL PATHS TO PROTECTION.

MOSQUITOES ARE PESKY, BUT THEY ATTACK FOR A REASON. IF YOU KNOW WHAT THEY'RE AFTER, YOU CAN STAY ONE STEP AHEAD!

SOLUTIONS!

# SOLUTIONS

Challenge #10: Create Clothing to Protect You From Mosquitoes

## >> GHOULISH GARB

JEFF
Geobiologist

### DESCRIBE YOUR SOLUTION.

I'll have to mix Halloween with Pirate Parrrrrty Day and go as a ghost pirate! I'll keep the hook and bandanna for after I come back to life as a pirate. For now, I'll grab a white sheet from the bed and toss it over my head to walk through the swarm. It will be effective because it covers my whole body, providing a barrier between the mosquitoes and me. Also, the sheet is a sort of invisibility cloak to a lot of insects, which are less attracted to white than to more vibrant colors.

### WHAT WERE YOUR FIRST THOUGHTS WHEN YOU READ THE CHALLENGE?

I could wear protective clothes or find a way to distract them in a different part of the yard. My solution might make me less visible to the insects in the first place, and it provides a barrier in case they come to investigate my bizarre costume.

### WHAT OTHER SOLUTIONS DID YOU CONSIDER?

I also thought of a few different costume-based ideas. Chain mail? Too hot, and more medieval knight than swashbuckling pirate. The crocodile that chased Captain Hook around Neverland? Could work, but green is more visible to insects than white.

## LAYER UP

**ERIKA**
*Deep-Sea Submersible Pilot*

**WHAT WAS YOUR FIRST IDEA? WAS IT YOUR BEST ONE?**

My first thought was to wrap myself in a big sheet and tape it closed. This wasn't the best choice because a mosquito can bite through thin material. My most usable idea was to drape netting around my pirate hat and wear thick linen pants taped tight at the ankles. A long-sleeve shirt with a thick vest and two hooks for hands would keep me mosquito-proof.

**WHAT WERE YOUR CRITERIA FOR A SUCCESSFUL SOLUTION?**

My clothing needed to be thick enough to thwart mosquito bites, but it also had to look awesome for my pirate party. Wearing a long-sleeve button-up shirt would provide protection but still make me look like a mariner. A successful solution would also allow me to see where I was going! Draping netting across my face kept the mosquitoes off my skin without blocking my vision.

## OUTSIDE THE BOX, INSIDE THE HOUSE

**RYAN**
*Coral Reef Biologist*

**DESCRIBE YOUR SOLUTION.**

Why move the party outside? It could be just as fun (and safe) to have my guests still come in. Guests arriving at the party would find a selection of jumpsuits made of a water-resistant material. The suits, which could be tightly sealed at the wrists and other openings, would prevent mosquito entry. Face protection, in the form of fencing masks, would be decorated to look like diver suits from the 1800s. Once dressed, guests would see signs indicating arrival at the "underwater world" and walk through a marine-themed display near the swarm. Then, guests would reach the house and have the option of changing out of the costume gear.

**WHAT WAS YOUR FIRST IDEA? WAS IT YOUR BEST ONE?**

My first idea was to arrange for everyone to wear costumes with thick fabric that fully covered the arms and legs, to protect most parts of the body. This was not my best idea. The guests would be hot and uncomfortable most of the day and their faces would still be exposed to bites. I also considered placing mesh nets around the swarm area to create a barrier between the mosquitoes and party guests. I rejected this solution because it would take a fair amount of work to enclose the territory with mesh. There would be no way to guarantee mosquitoes wouldn't escape, nor that they were all inside the net zone before the mesh went up.

More Solutions

# SOLUTIONS

THE NAT GEO ENGINEERS WERE REALLY BUZZING ABOUT THIS ONE! THEY SURE FOUND A FEW SOLUTION GEMS.

Challenge #10: Create Clothing to Protect You From Mosquitoes

MESH—OR A VEIL—CAN PROTECT YOUR FACE WITHOUT BLOCKING YOUR EYESIGHT.

If you can stretch the theme to cover Victorian-era costumes, you might be able to steal your sister's ballet tutu and use it to help protect your face.

MIKE

LOTS OF LAYERS KEEP YOU MOSQUITO FREE (AND ADD TO YOUR PIRATE PERSONA)!

TOM

I'm gonna throw a curve ball answer out there and say forget the clothes ... try smoke! Mosquitoes hate it!

DON'T TRY LIGHTING A TORCH IN REAL LIFE! YOU NEVER KNOW HOW FIRE AND MATERIALS WILL REACT.

A pirate-y torch! Pirates always have torches to go into caves and get their treasure.

TOM

# THE CHALLENGE

## COUSIN CONTAINMENT

### OBJECTIVE: BUILD AN OUTDOOR PLAY STRUCTURE

## The Situation

Your aunts and uncles are coming to visit, and this means an invasion of many little cousins. The only way to stop the tots from tearing through your treasures is to keep them outside. The only problem is you don't have a backyard playground. What super-duper fun and original play structure can you build that will keep them entertained for hours?

HEY! THIS LOOKS LIKE A BASKET! ANYONE HAVE A BALL?

TRY AN APPROACH THAT WILL PROVIDE MORE THAN ONE WAY TO HAVE FUN.

SOLUTIONS!

# SOLUTIONS

Challenge #11: Build an Outdoor Play Structure

**JOAN**
Author

## >> READY, SET, LIMBO!

When writing this challenge, I thought the Explorers would find ways to duplicate playground equipment using garage items. Once I started thinking of ideas, it was hard to stop!

The trick with this challenge is to make sure the solution will provide entertainment for hours. It needs to allow for different ages, interests, and abilities. My best solution for keeping a group of kids entertained for hours is to make the backyard into an obstacle course that can be changed throughout the day.

Here's my recipe. Tack two strips of survey tape into the ground to mark the start and finish lines. Arrange a series of firewood logs to jump over, tires for jumping in and out of, and—if you've got a tree—a rope to swing over a low-spraying sprinkler. Add a broom to be balanced upside down while walking as many steps as the player's age. Fix a basket at an angle and provide balled-up socks for tossing. Play jazzy music,

suspend a pole between a couple trees, and add limbo dancing to the course. Line up sawhorses to crawl under, and add a narrow board or wide cable to the ground for a low-level balancing challenge.

It's easy to make this activity last for hours. Hang up a poster listing each person's name, use a stopwatch to time first tries, and record the results. Now challenge the tots to beat their best times.

This solution works because firewood, a broom, balled-up socks, and the other obstacle course objects are not usually used as toys. That makes playing with them a fresh new experience. Using objects in unexpected ways surprises and entertains. Just like a real playground, though, it's important to check safety before use. Ask a grown-up to be your safety inspector, then get playing!

RYAN
Coral Reef Biologist

### DESCRIBE YOUR SOLUTION.

I realized the solution would have to inspire creativity—a trait that makes it possible for any activity to be enjoyed for hours. I decided to collect up to 50 cube-shaped cardboard boxes, tape each one of them completely closed, and paint them in different, bright colors. The kids would be able to select colors, make patterns, and build anything they could imagine in the backyard. The giant blocks would encourage them to use their imaginations and building skills, and keep them happily entertained for hours.

### WHY DID YOU CHOOSE THESE SPECIFIC MATERIALS AND TOOLS?

The solution uses materials that could be put together and taken down very quickly if necessary. The benefits of using boxes, tape, and paint are that these items are common household items and inexpensive. I chose boxes made of cardboard not sturdy enough to hold a child's weight to deter climbing on the creations. The fragility of the design is a potential problem because it will only work in dry weather.

## AMAZING OBSTACLES

MUNAZZA
Astronomer

### DESCRIBE YOUR SOLUTION.

I'd build the ultimate backyard obstacle course! I can arrange the potted plants in such a way that the cousins could weave through or jump over them. Then I'd turn the unused pots upside down so that the kids could use them as stepping-stones. Next I could create a "chair tunnel" by arranging two chairs to be tilted slightly on the rear legs with their seat backs touching. The kids could crawl through. I could also make a slide for a ball. I'd undo half of the ropes on the right-hand side of the laundry drying rack and anchor those ropes to the ground in a sloping fashion. Then, I'd tie a blanket on top to create a slide! To get the ball on the slide, I'd fashion a "buddy pulley system": I'd tie a rope to the basket and toss it over the left edge of the laundry rack. A buddy would need to pull the rope to hoist the ball in the basket up to the top. Then let the ball go! If the first obstacle course gets boring, we can change the order (or difficulty!) of challenges to keep the kids entertained!

### WHAT WERE YOUR FIRST THOUGHTS WHEN YOU READ THE CHALLENGE?

I was stumped when I first looked at the available materials—how could I keep the tots busy for hours with potted plants and a basket?! It was the structure in the back of the yard that really caught my attention, though, and got me thinking about a backyard obstacle course!

More Solutions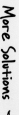

# SOLUTIONS

THE NAT GEO ENGINEERS REALLY USED THEIR IMAGINATIONS (AND GOT IN TOUCH WITH THEIR INNER TOTS) FOR THIS ONE!

Challenge #11: Build an Outdoor Play Structure

YOU CAN ROUND UP MATERIALS FROM YOUR GARAGE OR ART SUPPLY CLOSET, OR FIND THINGS HANGING AROUND THE HOUSE.

TOM

Cardboard boxes, markers, imagination ... that's all you need.

You can also pretend the cardboard box is the cockpit of an airplane.

BRAD

TAPE CARDBOARD BOXES TOGETHER TO FORM A TUNNEL.

Tape a bunch of boxes together to make a really long tunnel. Cut windows out and drop action figures through the openings as the kids crawl through the tunnel.

MIKE

CUT OUT WINDOWS.

If you know toddlers, you know they're really easy to keep entertained. You could literally throw a blanket over chairs. BOOM! Hours of fun!

ERIC

# THE CHALLENGE

## KEEP THE CHANGE

### OBJECTIVE: MAKE A COIN SORTER

### The Situation

Your family held a yard sale on the weekend and finally someone noticed how much you helped out. You get to keep all the change, but there are conditions. You have to put 80 percent of it in your savings account, and it's got to be rolled up for the bank before it opens at 10 a.m. tomorrow. There's got to be a way of counting your cash that's more fun than sifting through quarters and dimes. How can you sort your coins quickly?

# NUMBER 12

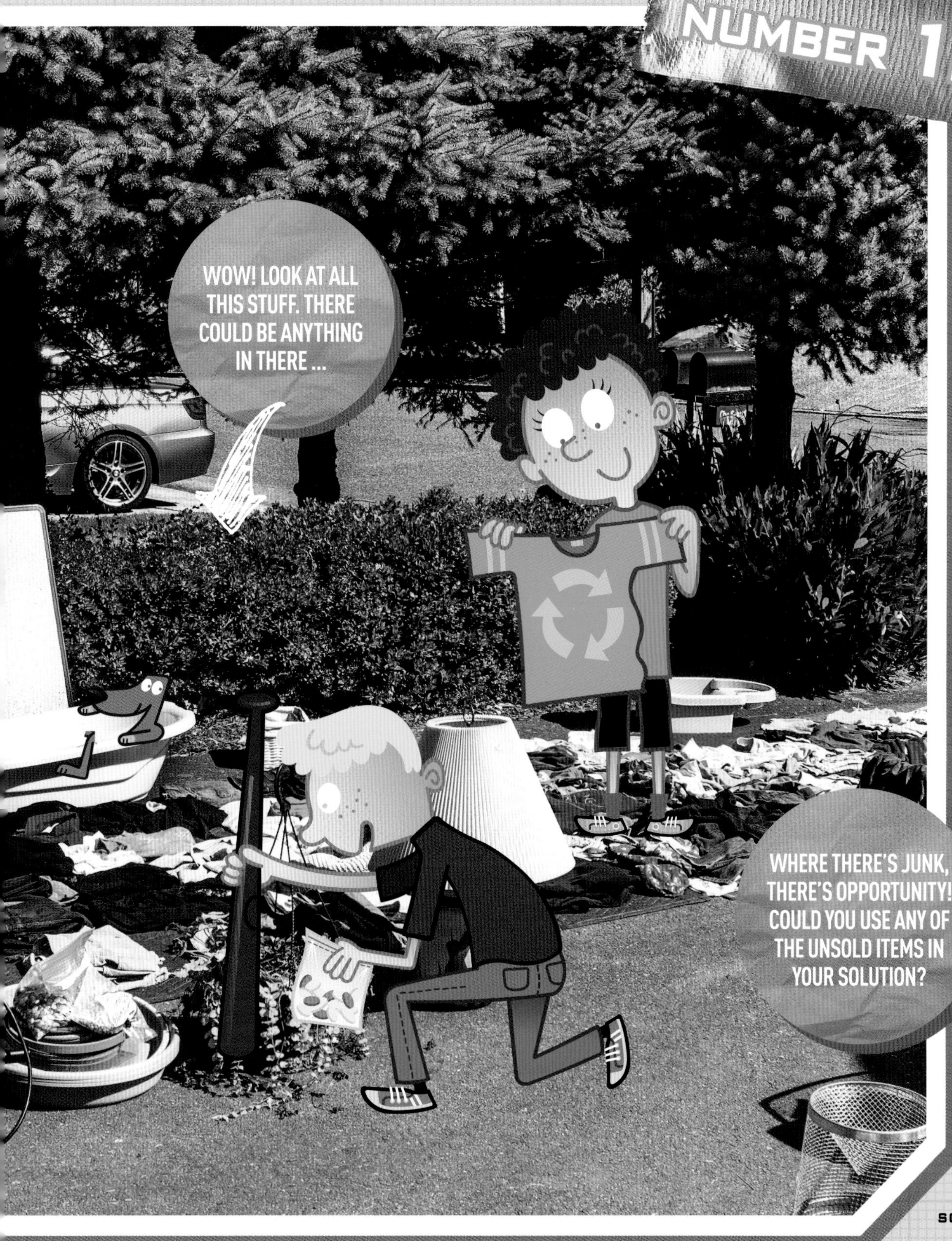


SOLUTIONS!

# SOLUTIONS

## Challenge #12: Make a Coin Sorter

**RYAN**
*Coral Reef Biologist*

## >> SLOT MACHINE

### DESCRIBE YOUR SOLUTION.

To count the change quickly, I would grab a roll of birthday present wrapping paper from the closet and remove the cardboard tube found inside. My next step would be to trace each coin type onto the cardboard and cut a hole, in order from smallest to largest. Each opening would be spaced equally along the tube's length. The tube would be secured at a 45-degree angle, perhaps on a piece of furniture or step stool, and an empty change roll placed under each of the holes. Sorting would involve slowly pouring the change through the center of the tube. Each piece of change would fall into its respective slot, with the larger coins sliding past the small holes.

I found that inserting too much change at one time created blockages and delayed sorting. This problem was overcome by limiting the number of coins I put in at one time. As well as preventing congestion, this took the stress off the flimsy materials. In choosing my final strategy, I considered what angle of ramp would work best. It had to allow the coins to move fast enough to overcome the cardboard's friction, but slow enough to fall through the different sizes of holes along its length. I took into account the coin's weight and what materials would be firm enough to support their weight, but remain easy to adjust and tweak based on the success of the sorting.

### WHAT WERE YOUR FIRST THOUGHTS WHEN YOU READ THE CHALLENGE?

My first idea was to separate the types of coin by weight and use some sort of spinning device that would cause the coins to separate by height. This was not my best idea because it was more complicated. I realized it would result in more mistakes and still involve manually adding each different type of coin. I wanted to create a method that would take less than an hour to set up and complete the sorting job in under an hour.

## PENNIED & DIMED

CINDY
Geologist

### DESCRIBE YOUR SOLUTION.

Fold a piece of cardboard into a V and cut some holes in the bottom—just smaller than a quarter—to let smaller coins fall through but catch the quarters. Repeat with more cardboard, making holes of decreasing sizes to catch each size of coin. You could also create a system of sieves by nesting cardboard Vs inside one another. When the change goes through the first "sieve," the quarters are caught in the cardboard, but the rest of the change drops into the next piece of cardboard. Its holes stop nickels, the next piece stops pennies, and the next stops dimes.

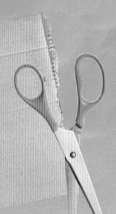

### HOW COULD YOUR SOLUTION BE USED FOR A REAL-WORLD PROBLEM?

In geology, shaking an item through a sieve is a standard technique that we use to sort sediments by their grain size (diameter). A sieve can be used to sort various items of different sizes, such as produce and eggs, for supermarkets.

## GO WITH THE FLOW

JEFF
Geobiologist

### DESCRIBE YOUR SOLUTION.

Sorting naturally happens in a mountain stream as the smallest particles, like pebbles and sand, wash to flatter areas where the water flow is slower. This happens because different rocks need different amounts of energy to move, depending on their size. I'd use this same principle to sort the coins, which all have different masses and will travel different lengths when moved by flowing water. I'll place all the coins on a gentle slope, like a driveway, and pour several buckets of water over them. Quarters should move the least, while dimes will move the farthest!

### WHAT WAS YOUR FIRST IDEA? WAS IT YOUR BEST ONE?

My breakfast cereal inspired my first idea. In most cereal boxes, all of the small bits fall to the bottom, between the spaces left by the larger pieces. Could the same principle work by shaking up a box of coins? Maybe, but probably not too well, because the sorting works best with rounder objects of very different masses and sizes.

### WHAT WERE YOUR CRITERIA FOR A SUCCESSFUL SOLUTION?

Complete separation of the four coin types would mean success but also be a lot of work. I'd rather use a time management strategy to get most of the way there in a short amount of time.

More Solutions

# SOLUTIONS

THE NAT GEO ENGINEERS CAME UP WITH A SOLUTION THAT YOU MIGHT SAY IS FULL OF HOLES ...

Challenge #12: Make a Coin Sorter

PULL ONE OF EACH TYPE OF COIN FROM YOUR HAUL AND ARRANGE THEM FROM LARGEST TO SMALLEST. THEN MEASURE EACH.

I'd take a bucket and make holes just smaller than a quarter. Then I'd put all the coins in the bucket and shake until every coin smaller than a quarter falls through the holes.

ERIC

A. 5¢ < ⟨⟩ < 25¢

B. 1¢ < ⟨⟩ < 5¢

C. 10¢ < ⟨⟩ < 1¢

MAKE HOLES IN THE BUCKET—ONE EACH JUST SMALLER THAN A QUARTER, A NICKEL, AND A PENNY.

Now make holes just smaller than a nickel to collect all the nickels. Keep making holes just smaller than the coin you are collecting until all the coins are separated.

BRAD

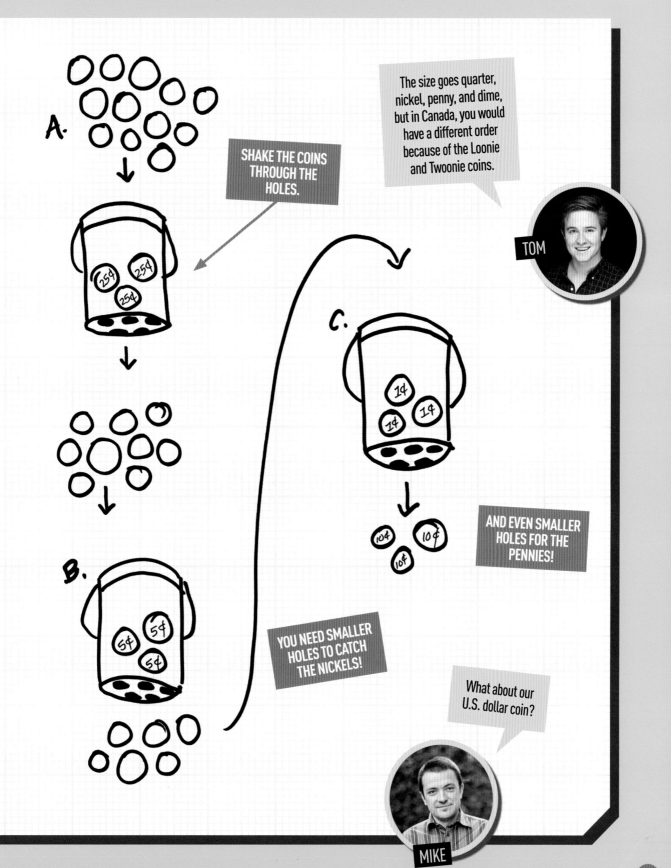

# THE CHALLENGE

## IT'S LIKE AN OVEN OUT HERE

**OBJECTIVE:** BAKE APPLES USING THE SUN

### The Situation

It's the hottest summer on record and it's been nine days since you've seen a cloud in the sky. It's your turn to make dessert, but Mom says it's too hot to use the kitchen oven. Still, you're dying to show off your recipe for killer baked apples. How do you cook your apple masterpiece using only the sun for energy?

YOU'VE ALREADY GOT ONE INGREDIENT—THE SUN!

DON'T FORGET THE OVEN MITTS! IF YOU DO IT RIGHT, THE PAN WILL BE HOT!

TINFOIL

YOU CAN DO MORE WITH TINFOIL THAN WRAP UP YOUR LEFTOVERS ...

SOLUTIONS!

# SOLUTIONS

Challenge #13: Bake Apples Using the Sun

## >> FOIL THE HEAT

**JOAN**
Author

Aluminum foil is so easy to work with, I expected it would appear in most of the solutions. As I wrote this challenge, I pictured people turning metal rain barrels into ovens and shaping pizza boxes into ovens. My own solution started with making a list of objects in the house or garage that could hold, magnify, or reflect heat:

1. Aluminum foil
2. Cast-iron frying pan
3. Magnifying glass
4. Metal colander
5. Aquarium
6. Metal vegetable steamer
7. Transparent milk jug filled with water
8. Windshield sunshade
9. Insulated lunch kit
10. Insulated mug
11. Pie plates
12. Cookie sheets
13. Water
14. Satellite dish
15. Plastic wrap
16. Mini garden greenhouse

Reviewing the list, I think about combining items to make the hottest oven. My first step is to wrap the apples in foil, shiny side inward to keep heat reflecting toward the food. I place the apples in a small cast-iron frying pan because the dense iron will absorb and hold heat. The pan goes in the aquarium, the aquarium goes in the satellite dish, and the mini garden greenhouse goes over top. I stack pie plates beneath one side of the satellite dish to angle it toward the sun.

This might be enough to cook the apples, but I'm quite hungry. Perhaps I can speed up the process by positioning more reflective objects around the oven. I prop the metallic windshield sunshade and cookie sheets against the chair legs. I take a couple umbrellas, wrap them in foil, and arrange them to focus sunlight toward the oven. Finally I take a roll of plastic kitchen wrap and loop it over and around the umbrellas and chairs to make an oven within an oven. Yikes, I've used a lot of materials for this solution! I wonder if Mom will ever ask me to cook again.

# OPTICAL OVEN

**RYAN**
Coral Reef Biologist

### DESCRIBE YOUR SOLUTION.

I would cook the apples using optics and geometry. First I would go outside and pick the sunniest spot on the hot asphalt driveway leading up to the house. Then I would set up several mirrors to angle the midday sun toward one central point, where the cooking would take place. The reflected outdoor light would cook my killer baked apples without adding heat inside the house. At first it was difficult to achieve a high enough temperature to cook the recipe. I solved this by adding more mirrors to the setup. I wanted to make sure the recipe would taste the same as it does when baked normally in the kitchen oven.

### WHY DID YOU CHOOSE THESE SPECIFIC MATERIALS AND TOOLS?

For my solution to be successful, I needed several mirrors and a black asphalt surface to obtain the maximum heat possible during the midday sun. A benefit of these materials is that they are commonplace and inexpensive. The downside is that it is incredibly difficult to obtain a precise temperature at the focal point of the mirrors, and the entire system is dependent on the weather. Had I chosen to cook the apples in a campfire pit in the backyard, I would have needed enough wood, paper, and twigs to start and sustain the fire.

# SIDEWALK SWEETS

**DENISE**
Archaeologist

### DESCRIBE YOUR SOLUTION.

My solution is to cook the apples in a foil oven, right on the sidewalk. Begin by wrapping each apple in aluminum foil. Place them on a metal tray and cover the top of the tray with a layer of foil. The whole setup should be placed on the pavement, ideally during the hottest hours of the day, around noon.

### WHY DID YOU CHOOSE THESE SPECIFIC MATERIALS AND TOOLS?

I chose the metal trays and aluminum foil because they will increase the heat at surface level and should be enough to cook the apples thoroughly. I put them on the concrete floor because I have seen people frying eggs on the pavement on hot days, so I know it can get hot enough to provide enough heat from both the bottom and the top to ensure thorough cooking.

### HOW COULD YOUR SOLUTION BE USED FOR A REAL-WORLD PROBLEM?

This solution could be used to boil unclean water in hot places where there is difficulty accessing potable water.

More Solutions

THE NAT GEO ENGINEERS DON'T MESS AROUND WHEN IT COMES TO FOOD. THEY KNOW THERE'S MORE THAN ONE WAY TO COOK AN APPLE.

Challenge #13: Bake Apples Using the Sun

ALUMINUM FOIL!

glass/windowpane

①

MIKE

Find a wooden box. A metal one would be better, but wood is fine. Put the apple in the box, then get a bunch of cardboard covered in foil and point that toward the food.

COVER FOUR CARDBOARD FLAPS IN ALUMINUM FOIL AND ANGLE THEM TOWARD THE APPLE.

Sounds delicious!

BRAD

PLACE THE APPLE IN A METAL POT

MIKE

You need a window on top of the box. The light from the sun passes through the glass and turns into heat energy, which can't escape the glass as easily. To make it hotter, you'd want a bunch of reflective stuff.

PUT THE APPLE AND POT INSIDE THE BOX.

THE WINDOWPANE GOES BETWEEN YOUR APPLE AND THE SUN.

Instead of foil, ideally, you could temporarily borrow all of the small, personal mirrors from the house ...

ERIC

# THE CHALLENGE

## TACO TROUBLE

### OBJECTIVE: REMOVE HOT PEPPER SAUCE FROM THE SWIMMING POOL

### The Situation

You invite the gang over for a swimming party but break the golden rule of the pool: Never eat in the water. You're pouring hot pepper sauce onto your taco when a beach ball smacks you in the forehead. The jumbo-size jar tips and sauce spreads through the once clear water. How can you get rid of the hot sauce without draining the pool?

WHAT'S THE HOT SAUCE MADE OUT OF? THAT COULD BE IMPORTANT. AND YOU'LL PROBABLY WANT TO GRAB A PAIR OF GOGGLES BEFORE GOING BACK INTO THE POOL.

# SOLUTIONS

Challenge #14: Remove Hot Pepper Sauce From the Swimming Pool

## ▶▶ DIVIDE AND CONQUER

**ERIKA**
Deep-Sea Submersible Pilot

### DESCRIBE YOUR SOLUTION.

Yikes! The first thing to do will be to keep the spill contained, *fast!* First I'd turn off the jets and pumps to keep water from mixing the sauce around. Next I'd make a containment boom by taping a pool noodle lengthwise along a towel. I'd dip the towel into the water on the outermost edge of the spill, curve the ends of the noodle toward the side of the pool, then stick the noodle to the edge of the pool with duct tape. I'd take the towel's bottom corners and slowly lift them up to the surface. The material is coated in sticky, wet taco sauce, but the water is (mostly) clean!

### WHY DID YOU CHOOSE THESE SPECIFIC MATERIALS AND TOOLS?

I didn't have to leave home to clean up the mess! A towel, pool noodle, and duct tape are common items. Using readily available materials made it possible to build the containment barrier fast enough to contain the spill. Since the taco sauce is water-soluble, it spreads in water. Even though the oil in it separates and is fairly easy to scoop off the top, the vinegar and pepper ingredients would have been very difficult to filter if they had spread into the entire body of water. The noodle was vital to stopping that from happening. Another option was baking soda, which could be poured onto the spill to neutralize the acidic taco sauce. I also thought about trying to use a shop vac, which can filter water, but the volume of water was too great.

### HOW COULD YOUR SOLUTION BE USED FOR A REAL-WORLD PROBLEM?

Containment booms are used in oil spills. When an oil drill in the ocean breaks and oil gushes into the water, the crew rapidly deploys an oilproof net to stop oil from leaking outside the immediate spill area.

## SUPER SCOOPER

**RYAN**
Coral Reef Biologist

### WHAT WAS YOUR FIRST IDEA? WAS IT YOUR BEST ONE?

My first idea was to remove the sauce from the water with something like a coffee filter inside of a strainer. I don't think it was my best plan. It would take quite a lot of time to siphon enough water to remove all of the sauce from the pool, and it might not be effective if the sauce was too thick or the filter got too wet. Instead, my solution would be to tape enough pool noodles together to span the width of the entire pool. The noodles could be pushed across the water to contain the spill in one area, making it easy to collect the sauce with a pool skimmer or bucket.

### WHAT WERE YOUR CRITERIA FOR A SUCCESSFUL SOLUTION?

1) Enough sauce was removed to ensure the pool filter didn't become clogged.
2) The water didn't smell like sauce or sting the eyes more than usual.
3) The materials used were easily found near the pool.
4) Most of the pool's original water was retained.

## QUICK THINKING

**CINDY**
Geologist

### DESCRIBE YOUR SOLUTION.

Empty the air out of the beach ball and make a small hole on the side opposite the air nozzle. Put your mouth on the beach ball's air nozzle and aim the hole at the contaminated water. Inhale to create suction, then suck the hot sauce and contaminated water into the beach ball. Remove the ball from the pool and dump out the contaminated water. Repeat as needed.

### WHAT WERE YOUR FIRST THOUGHTS WHEN YOU READ THE CHALLENGE?

At first I wasn't sure how to handle the problem, but I kept thinking about what materials were around the pool and how they could be most helpful for a quick and easy solution. I ran through my head what the scenario would look like, and kept rereading the question.

### WHAT OTHER SOLUTIONS DID YOU CONSIDER?

I thought of grabbing a towel and trying to soak up the contaminated pool water. I knew this would only work if the hot sauce stayed in a small, concentrated area, not if it spread throughout the entire pool. It took me about 10 minutes of thinking before I came to my best solution!

More Solutions

# NAT GEO ENGINEER SOLUTIONS

THE NAT GEO ENGINEERS REALLY DOVE INTO THIS ONE! TWO FAVORITE IDEAS BUBBLED TO THE TOP: ISOLATING THE SPILL TO SUCK IT OUT OF THE POOL AND MAKING A MAKESHIFT EXTRA-STRENGTH FILTER.

## Challenge #14: Remove Hot Pepper Sauce From the Swimming Pool

**TOSS FLOAT RING OVER SPILL**

My idea, well, you're in a swimming pool, so you're going to have floaty toys. If you have access to a floaty ring, throw that over the spill to contain it.

**GET OUT OF THE POOL OR GET SOME GOGGLES! YOU DON'T WANT HOT SAUCE IN YOUR EYES. TRUST US!**

BRAD

**SLURP TACO SAUCE THROUGH STRAW**

Then use a straw to suck up the part of the pepper sauce that's floating.*

Right. The only part of the pepper sauce people will see is the oily part floating on the surface. That's the part with the red pepper flakes. The rest of the sauce is colorless. It will sink into the pool water and disperse.

*Be sure you don't let it get all the way to your mouth! The chemicals in the pool aren't good for drinking.

ERIC

The solution to pollution is dilution.

USE PILLOW STUFFING TO FILTER SAUCE

Another thing you could do is build a superstrong filter using charcoal. Take a five-gallon (19-L) bucket and poke a hole near the bottom of the bucket so the newly cleaned water will be able to drain back into the pool.

MIKE

USE CHARCOAL TO PURIFY WATER

POKE HOLE IN BUCKET

Put a small pillow or cushion at the bottom of the bucket. That will prevent charcoal from getting into the pool. Now top the bucket with charcoal and put the bucket on the edge of the pool. Make a siphon by putting one end of some clean tubing in the pool and sucking on the other end to get the flow started. Direct the water through the filter and watch as hot sauce water flows into the bucket and clean water flows back into the pool.

REDIRECT WATER THROUGH EMERGENCY FILTER

Couldn't we just blame a younger sibling?

TOM

125

# ENGINEERING OUR WORLD

Warning!
You might just be
inspired to change
the world.

# ENGINEERING SUCCESSES
## OVER THE CENTURIES

**SURE, THE CHALLENGES IN THIS BOOK ARE WACKY.**
Will you really need to thwart thirstiness in the desert? Likely not. But humans have faced all kinds of challenges throughout history, and every time, it's been engineering to the rescue.

# ANCIENT TIMES

**HUMANS' FIRST TOOLS WERE SIMPLE,** but without centuries of people building upon them, civilization could not have advanced to where it is today. Early engineers used complex math to develop their ideas. They built great structures that still exist today—thousands of years later. Their imaginative use of the Earth's resources changed the world.

## The wheel

Type of Engineering:
### MECHANICAL

The wheel has been described as the greatest invention of all time. It changed transportation forever and is still being used today. Invented around 3500 B.C., the first wheel was made in Mesopotamia (an ancient Middle East region now including parts of Iraq, Iran, Syria, and Turkey).

Archaeologists in the United Kingdom unearth a 3,000-year-old wheel.

## The seeder plow

Type of Engineering:
### MECHANICAL/ AGRICULTURAL

The seeder plow changed agriculture by making it possible to plow and plant seeds at the same time. This important piece of technology allowed farmers to plant faster, waste less seed, and grow larger crops. The Mesopotamians were using plows by 3000 B.C.

## The Great Pyramids

Type of Engineering:
### CIVIL/ARCHITECTURAL

The pyramids on the Giza Plateau in Egypt were built more than 4,500 years ago. It took about 80 years and millions of large stone blocks to build one pyramid. Each stone, weighing from about 2.5 to 15 tons (2.3 to 13.6 t), was set in place with more precision than modern stoneworkers use today. Scientists know stone picks, copper chisels, and other primitive tools were used, but they are unable to fully explain how the pyramids were built.

## The Great Sphinx

Type of Engineering:
### CIVIL/ARCHITECTURAL

The Great Sphinx is one of the oldest statues in the world, built around 2500 B.C. An engineering marvel carved using hand tools from a single section of limestone, the Sphinx has the face of a man and the body of a lion. Its paws are the length of a city bus. Standing as tall as the White House in Washington, D.C., it's about 66 feet (20 m) high and 240 feet (73 m) long. During the building process, it would have taken one person 40 hours to remove a single cubic foot (.03 cubic m) of stone.

## The Parthenon

**AN ALMOST** PERFECT **REPLICA** OF THE **PARTHENON CAN BE** FOUND IN NASHVILLE, TENNESSEE, U.S.A.

*The Parthenon, Greece*

Type of Engineering: **CIVIL/ARCHITECTURAL**

The Parthenon in Athens, Greece, is a 2,500-year-old temple made from marble blocks. The engineers used optical tricks to make it appear perfectly proportioned and straight. The quality of the temple's construction and its beauty make it a masterpiece, even in its current condition as a ruin.

## The Great Wall of China

Type of Engineering: **CIVIL**

The Great Wall of China is a network of walls built by emperors from time periods that span more than 2,000 years. The wall was built to keep invaders out and citizens in. It stretches 4,000 miles (6,400 km) across northern China—about the same distance as New York City to Alaska, U.S.A. Built by hand, it stretches from two to three highway lanes wide and rises as high as a three-story building.

## Roman aqueducts and sewer systems

Type of Engineering: **CIVIL**

Many ancient civilizations engineered ways to transport water so that they could live and farm farther away from natural water sources. Ancient Rome is especially known for its aqueducts, which extended 280 miles (450 km). The first was built in 312 B.C. and the last in A.D. 226. Gravity, not pressure, allowed the water to flow along stone- or concrete-lined trenches, both above and below the ground. Archways and bridges were used to maintain the desired slope.

Ancient Rome's main waste- and storm-water drainage line, the Cloaca Maxima, was built in the sixth century B.C. It's still used to transport runoff, although concrete has been used to replace much of the original stonework.

# MIDDLE AGES 5TH–15TH CENTURIES

**THE TERM "ENGINEER" WAS FIRST USED IN THE MIDDLE AGES,** a time when engineering advances were often practical. There was little growth in scientific knowledge in the Western world, but progress was made in developing labor-saving machines and devices, from spinning wheels to ship rudders.

## The flying buttress

### Type of Engineering: CIVIL

Before the flying buttress was invented in 12th-century France, stone walls were used to support heavy roofs. The flying buttress transformed architecture by allowing engineers to build higher walls and use other materials, like glass. Cathedrals and other buildings became less dark and more beautiful. The buttress is called "flying" because its arch extends or "flies" a distance away from the wall. It carries the roof's weight through its stonework to the ground.

## The drawbridge

### Type of Engineering: CIVIL

Medieval-age castle dwellers tried to discourage enemy attacks by building deep moats around outer walls. They crossed moats on drawbridges—movable platforms that could be lifted to stop invaders from getting in. Raised bridges covered castle entrances and provided extra protection from battering rams and catapult-fired rocks.

# Waterwheels

### Type of Engineering: MECHANICAL

Before steam power was invented, waterwheels provided an important source of mechanical energy. Flowing water turned large wheels, usually to grind grain into flour—a job that had been done by hand for thousands of years. By the end of the 10th century, waterwheels were used to crush ore, power forges to shape metal, and provide energy for many other jobs. Building these enormous structures in medieval times took remarkable feats of engineering.

# Windmills

### Type of Engineering: MECHANICAL

The invention of mechanical windmills forever changed the way work was done. Like waterwheels, windmills were used for grinding grain, but they had advantages over waterwheels. They cost less to build and could be erected away from water. Windmills were common in Europe from the 12th to the 19th centuries.

# Trebuchets

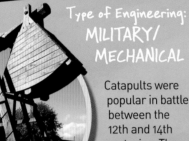

### Type of Engineering: MILITARY/ MECHANICAL

Catapults were popular in battles between the 12th and 14th centuries. The trebuchet was a powerful type of catapult that could be shot with great accuracy. Its power came from massive counterweights—some as heavy as 10 tons (9 t). The weapon was usually used to hurl rocks at castle walls, but burning objects were sometimes launched to spread fire. The bodies of plague victims and rotting animals were also shot to spread disease to enemies. The largest trebuchet ever built may have been the War Wolf (pictured above), made in Scotland in 1304. It took three months to build and perhaps 50 men or more to operate. The engineers who designed these weapons were well respected.

BUILT IN 1665, OUTWOOD MILL IN GREAT BRITAIN WAS STILL A WORKING MILL UNTIL 1996. **THAT'S 331 YEARS OF MEDIEVAL TECHNOLOGY AT WORK!**

## Clocks

### Type of Engineering: MECHANICAL

Imagine what it would be like to never know the time, or to live in the 10th century, when people carried pocket sundials! The first mechanical clocks were made around A.D. 1275. They worked using gears, weights, and levers held in tall clock towers. Hammers struck bells at regular intervals to announce the hour. The first clocks had no faces or hands to indicate the hour because few people knew how to read numbers. Clock building took a long time. Every part, from screws to springs, had to be made by hand.

The first water clock to indicate hours and minutes was made in Cairo, Egypt, by a scientist named Al-Hasan Ibn al-Haytham. His invention involved a cylinder with a small hole in it, which measured time by sinking into a tank of water. It used a pulley and other mechanical parts to turn a circular disc and show the time.

THE SALISBURY CATHEDRAL MEDIEVAL CLOCK IN WILTSHIRE, ENGLAND, MAY BE THE OLDEST WORKING CLOCK THAT STILL EXISTS. BELIEVED TO HAVE BEEN BUILT IN 1386 OR EARLIER, THE CLOCK MUST BE WOUND ONCE A DAY.

MUCH LIKE A RUBE GOLDBERG INVENTION, THE ELEPHANT CLOCK PROVIDED ENTERTAINMENT BY CAUSING A VARIETY OF SOUNDS AND MOVEMENTS.

## THE GOLDEN AGE OF MUSLIM CIVILIZATION
### (7TH–16TH CENTURIES)

WHILE EUROPE EXPERIENCED THE DARK AGES, an era of great achievement was taking place in a vast area stretching from southern Spain to China. During the Golden Age of Muslim Civilization, Arabic became the international language of science. Scholars traveled to share information and ideas, and women and men from different faiths and cultures worked together to gain and expand their knowledge. Advances in science, technology, engineering, mathematics, and many other fields are rooted in this ancient era.

## THE ELEPHANT CLOCK

The Elephant Clock is a water-powered clock, created in the 13th century by Al-Jazari, a renowned engineer from Turkey. A work of art as well as a timepiece, it used the descent of a bowl in a hidden tank of water to track time. The bowl, which took half an hour to sink, triggered a ball to turn a dial to show the hour. The sinking bowl also pulled ropes that caused a scribe and his pen to turn and show the minutes past the hour.

# SCIENTIFIC REVOLUTION

**THE SCIENTIFIC REVOLUTION WAS A PERIOD FROM THE 15TH TO 17TH CENTURIES IN WESTERN CIVILIZATION WHEN GROWING KNOWLEDGE IN MATH AND SCIENCE LED TO NEW WAYS OF THINKING.**

The refinement of the scientific method—a standard process for conducting experiments—meant that scientists and other experts could prove their ideas and test each other's work. This was an important step toward the application of science in engineering.

In the 16th century, civil and military engineering were popular jobs. As texts were published on science, math, and machines, it became easier to share ideas and learn. Interest in problem solving grew and engineers developed power-driven machines. Factories began to replace work once done by hand, leading to the Industrial Revolution—a period that began in England in the 18th century and spread to the rest of the world.

## The lightning rod

### Type of Engineering: ELECTRICAL

Benjamin Franklin once studied a lightning storm by chasing it on horseback. Another time, he experienced an electrical shock during an experiment. This famous American scientist and inventor became the first to identify lightning as electricity. In 1752, Franklin built the first lightning rod to protect structures from lightning damage. His invention is still used today, with only minor changes to the original design.

Lightning rods are installed on the highest points of buildings or ships. The rod, usually made of copper, works by sending the lightning's current through cables to the ground. The rod helps prevent lightning from striking flammable materials and starting a fire. Cables provide lightning with the least resistant path to the ground.

## Parachutes

### Type of Engineering: AEROSPACE

Leonardo da Vinci—painter, inventor, and great thinker—imagined a parachute and drew a picture of his idea around 1485. More than 300 years later, André-Jacques Garnerin jumped from a hot-air balloon wearing a cotton parachute. It swung violently from side to side but brought him to the ground uninjured, though feeling quite ill. Jumping from hot-air balloons with parachutes strapped on became a form of entertainment in the 19th century. Parachutes later became important lifesaving devices for airplane crews, especially during the Second World War. Today parachutes are used in skydiving, as well as to slow the fall or speed of aircraft, spacecraft, race cars, or other objects.

# Hot-air balloons

### Type of Engineering: THERMAL/FLUID

The first hot-air balloon flights amazed spectators and frightened peasants who had not heard about the invention. The Montgolfier brothers invented balloon flight in France, in 1783. Their first balloon was made of cloth panels, lined with paper and buttoned together. It used burning straw to create hot air. The heated air, less dense than the surrounding air, caused the balloon to float upward.

The balloon inspired others, and the physicist Jacques Alexandre César Charles designed a balloon fueled by hydrogen, a gas lighter than air. The gas balloon rose by pushing the heavier air out of the way. Modern balloons are used for recreation and to study weather high above the Earth.

# The cotton gin and interchangeable parts

### Type of Engineering: MECHANICAL

Before cloth can be made from cotton, the seedpods must be removed from the fiber. This tedious work was done by hand until an American, Eli Whitney, invented the first cotton gin in 1793. His machine lowered the cost of farming by making it easier to separate the cotton plant parts.

**ENGINEERING IS ADVANCING MORE QUICKLY THAN EVER BEFORE.** Computer software allows 21st-century engineers to make models of almost anything they can imagine. New technologies make it possible for engineers and scientists to work on new ideas with experts around the world.

## Technology you can wear

### Type of Engineering: SOFTWARE

Engineers have taken wearable technology beyond watches and hearing aids. Feel like working on your fitness? You can get bracelets that tell you how many steps you walk, the distance you travel, and how fast your heart is beating. Feel like making a video without holding a camera? You can get a wearable camera that straps to your head so you can record the view as you ski down a mountain, swim in a lake, or walk to school. And if you just want convenience, you can get a pair of glasses that takes pictures and accesses the Internet.

UN PANEL QUE PRODUCE AGUA POTABLE DEL AIRE ES INGENIO EN ACCIÓN.

AIRE

EXAMEN DE ADMISIÓN: 3 DE MARZO

H2O

UTEC
UNIVERSIDAD DE INGENIERÍA & TECNOLOGÍA

ClearChannel OUTDOOR

AGUA

AQUÍ

## Water-making billboard

### Type of Engineering: MECHANICAL/ HYDROLOGICAL

It almost never rains in the coastal desert city of Lima, and that leads to a shortage of drinking water. The University of Engineering and Technology of Peru and an ad agency worked together to show how the problem could be solved. Taking advantage of the 98 percent humidity in the air, they built a billboard that captures the moisture in the air and condenses it into drinking water. No rain clouds required.

ONE COMPANY IS USING 3-D PRINTERS TO PRINT MASSIVE PARTS FOR AIRPLANES.

# 3-D printer

### Type of Engineering:
## MECHANICAL/INDUSTRIAL

Three-dimensional printers are machines that use computer files to make 3-D objects. Printers may build with plastic, metal, or other materials, but they all "print" by layering a heated material to form an object. They can create almost anything you can draw, including complicated objects with moving parts. You can print things as simple as a cube or as complex as a guitar.

While 3-D technology is fun, it also plays an important role in making it easier and less expensive to build prototypes and test ideas. NASA is studying how items printed on the International Space Station (ISS) compare to those printed on Earth. The first tool printed in space, a ratchet wrench, was made in four hours. That's a lot faster and less costly than shipping a tool from Earth. NASA is looking at how 3-D printers in space might be used to print complicated tools, an entire spacecraft, or meals that could remain fresh for five years.

# Anti-graffiti coatings

### Type of Engineering:
## CHEMICAL

Anti-graffiti coatings and films are 21st-century solutions to the expensive problem of cleaning up graffiti in public places. Coatings have been engineered to stop paint from sticking to surfaces on commonly vandalized structures from buildings and bridges to bus shelters. Coatings are transparent, and different types are used to help prevent paint from penetrating materials like concrete, steel, plastics, and wood. Even glass can be protected from permanent ink and etching. A nearly invisible film is applied to the glass. Cleanup is easier and the film is much less expensive to replace than the glass.

## Self-driving cars

### Type of Engineering: AUTOMOTIVE

Self-driving cars could make road travel safer because, unlike human drivers, computers don't become distracted or make mistakes. A vehicle that drives itself uses cameras, radar, lasers, GPS, sensors, and other technologies to determine where it is, where it's going, and where it should be. A computer analyzes the information and tells the car what to do. Although driverless cars can operate with more information than the human mind can collect, there's still more work to do. Engineers need to perfect a car's ability to respond to the unexpected, to better mimic the way a human can respond.

## Flying cars

### Type of Engineering: AUTOMOTIVE/ AEROSPACE

Engineers are exploring designs that would make it possible for a car to fly. Imagine being able to rise above the traffic, literally. Flying cars would help reduce the congestion in cities. They could also allow people to "drive" to places otherwise inaccessible by road. But landing and takeoff are two problems engineers need to overcome. Flying vehicles must be able to rise up and set down like helicopters, rather than speed up and slow down on runways like airplanes.

## Self-healing concrete

### Type of Engineering: CIVIL

Can you imagine a crack in concrete that repairs itself? A Dutch scientist not only imagined it, he explored how to use bacteria to self-seal cracks in concrete. The bacteria can remain dormant for up to 200 years, then become active when water and nutrients enter a new crack. This technology could be used to prevent problems that occur when water leaks into concrete structures and damages steel reinforcements.

# Robots

### Type of Engineering: ROBOTICS

Robots are often designed to do jobs people don't like to do or cannot do, or work that needs to be done consistently over long periods of time. Engineers have created robots that can vacuum your house, mop your floor, and mow your lawn. They've even built robots that explore space—rovers, landers, and orbiters. Computers on Earth are used to send signals to these distant robots to tell them what actions to take.

Engineers have also created humanoid robots designed to play soccer and compete in an annual competition, the Robot Soccer World Cup. RoboCup organizers hope to see a robotic team that can play and beat humans in an official International Federation of Football (FIFA) game by 2050. Figuring out how to make the best soccer-playing robot is fun, but important, too. By developing soccer-playing robots, engineers are tackling tough problems. These include robotic vision, bipedal walking, and the ability to make independent decisions—a task that involves programming robot responses to every possible situation.

Discoveries may lead to humanoid robots that can sense their surroundings well enough to help elderly or disabled people manage household chores. This research could aid industry through the use of robots able to perform a variety of tasks well, instead of just one task. Humanoid robot research may also boost the abilities of robots used in rescue missions after explosions, hazardous chemical spills, and other disasters.

**CURIOSITY ROVER HAS 17 CAMERAS AND CAN EVEN TAKE SELFIES ON MARS!**

# ENGINEERING DISASTERS

**ENGINEERING FAILURES HAPPEN** FOR MANY REASONS, FROM **ERRORS IN DESIGN,** TO CHOICE OF MATERIALS, TO SEVERE WEATHER. JUST THINK OF **THE THREE LITTLE PIGS** AND THEIR HOUSES OF STRAW, STICKS, AND BRICKS. ONLY THE **PRACTICAL PIG** CHOSE A MATERIAL THAT COULD WITHSTAND HUFFING AND PUFFING.

**LIKE OUR LITTLE PIGGY FRIENDS, ENGINEERS NEED TO CONSIDER MANY "WHAT- IF" SCENARIOS WHEN DESIGNING STRUCTURES.** What if there's a hurricane, earthquake, or tsunami? Sometimes it takes a full-on failure for engineers to figure out the best solutions. Early engineers depended on trial and error—testing ideas and trying different approaches. Today, accidents can be prevented by using computer models to predict how structures will respond to weather and other variables. Engineering failures lead to better, safer ways of solving problems.

## The Truesdell Bridge failure

Bridges have been broken and destroyed by ships, landslides, storms, earthquakes, and excess weight. In 1873, more than 100 people in Dixon, Illinois, U.S.A., stood on a 660-foot (200-m)-long wagon and foot bridge. They were watching a baptism service in the Rock River when the four-year-old bridge suddenly collapsed beneath them. The disaster killed more than 40 people and injured many others. Its failure was blamed on the supporting structure—the cast-iron Truesdell truss. Disasters like this have led to better methods of predicting bridge strength and conducting stress tests.

## Tower of Pisa

The Leaning Tower of Pisa is an eight-story, freestanding bell tower in Italy. Its dome, arches, striped marble, and 207 columns make it a stunning piece of architecture. Construction began in 1173, but it took about 200 years to build this marvel of medieval engineering. Wars, a shortage of money, and that famous leaning problem interrupted work.

Built on soft ground, one side of the tower began to sink after the second story was built. Engineers tried to fix the problem by changing the design, but the tower continued to sink. In the late 20th century, it stood with a 16-foot (5-m) lean. In 1990, engineers began the 11-year project that reduced the tilt about 17 inches (43 cm). The leaning tower reminds designers how important it is to study underground water and soil layers before building new structures.

# The Titanic

The *Titanic* was the largest ship in the world when it was built, and rumor said it was unsinkable. On its first voyage, on April 14, 1912, the *Titanic* struck an iceberg. The ice tore a 300-foot (91-m) hole into the ship's side and water poured in—too fast to be stopped. In less than three hours, the luxury steamship that had taken three years to build broke in half and sank to the bottom of the North Atlantic Ocean. The ship held only 20 lifeboats instead of the 64 first planned. The engineers were so confident in the ship's safety, they opted to add fewer lifeboats in order to give first-class passengers more deck space.

It's believed the *Titanic* broke apart and sunk so fast mainly due to design errors. Bulkheads—walls that separate different areas—were lowered to make the ship more glamorous. This allowed water to spread and sink the ship more quickly. Poor materials were also a problem. The rivets used to connect metal to the ship's frame broke when the ice scraped against its side.

Two years after the disaster, maritime nations came together to create an international treaty on ship safety. It included rules about lifeboat design, the use of public address systems (the *Titanic* didn't have one), and distress alerts with better range (now managed with satellite technology).

AROUND 700 PEOPLE WERE RESCUED FROM THE ICY WATERS, BUT MORE THAN 1,500 PASSENGERS AND CREW LOST THEIR LIVES.

# ENGINEERING THE FUTURE

EVEN THOUGH WE'VE BECOME USED TO **RAPIDLY CHANGING** TECHNOLOGY, **IDEAS** FOR THE FUTURE CAN **SOUND LIKE SCIENCE FICTION. WHO KNOWS** WHICH OF THESE DESIGNS WILL BECOME NORMAL PARTS OF LIFE?

## Invisibility

Researchers are exploring ways to make an object invisible using meta-materials—engineered materials with qualities not usually found in nature. Early designs have shown invisibility is possible! Optical engineering and nanotechnology are used to hide an object by guiding the light around it. The light is bent in a way that allows background objects to still be seen.

## Fuel from seawater

Where do you gas up when you're far out at sea? Ships rely on tankers when it's time to refuel, but new technology may offer another choice. Researchers are experimenting with ways to create fuel from seawater. The process involves turning carbon dioxide and hydrogen gases in the seawater into liquid fuel.

## Supersonic air travel

Today's fastest passenger planes can reach 700 miles an hour (1,125 km/h). Supersonic passenger jets of the future may travel more than 1,800 miles an hour (3,000 km/h). That means you could travel from New York to Los Angeles in less than an hour.

## Orbiting solar panels

The atmosphere, clouds, seasons, and night reduce the amount of solar energy that can be collected from Earth. In space, none of these barriers exist. Placing solar panels in space could make it possible to collect energy from the sun, convert it into microwaves or lasers, and beam the power to electric grids on Earth.

## Roads that melt ice

Governments currently spend billions of dollars to clear snow off roads. Future sidewalks, streets, and highways could be made out of panels that harness solar energy. They would never form potholes, would stay warm enough to keep lanes clear of ice and snow, and would warn drivers of dangers ahead, such as car accidents or animals on the road.

# ENGINEERING NEVER ENDS

**ENGINEERS OF THE FUTURE** WILL USE THE SAME STEPS YOU AND OUR EXPLORERS TOOK TO **SOLVE PROBLEMS.** THEY WILL BRAINSTORM, TEST IDEAS, AND MAKE REVISIONS. THEY WILL **WONDER HOW THINGS COULD BE** AND USE THEIR IMAGINATIONS—AND THEIR MATH AND SCIENCE SKILLS—TO FIND OUT.

**YOU'VE SEEN THE STEPS THEY TAKE—FROM START TO SOLUTION**—one action leading to another to solve problems, create new things, and get work done. You may also have noticed engineering never ends. From past to present to future, there are always improvements to make and new ideas to explore.

You can use engineering to solve everyday problems too. Start by keeping track of all those little annoying things in your life. Consider the little things that happen over and over again—the ones you wish would just go away. You might get ideas by finishing the sentence "I can't stand it when ..."

## KEEP AN ONGOING LIST OF ANNOYING PET PEEVES.

Now, instead of suffering in silence (or loudly), seek solutions. Think about how you can follow the steps of engineering to overcome obstacles, eradicate the irritation, destroy the dilemma!

Remember, engineers build their skills by tackling small problems first, then working their way up to larger ones. After you make your list, do the same. Tackle straightforward problems first, then use your new skills to tackle the trickier ones.

>> How might you engineer a solution to these problems?

## Possible Problems to Solve

- You get a static electricity shock every time you cross a carpet.

- The zipper on your jacket won't stay up.

- After two bites, your ice pop breaks and hits the floor.

- The eraser on top of your pencil smears your writing.

- Your book won't stay open unless you hold both front and back covers.

- You break holes in your bread when spreading peanut butter on it.

- The banana in your backpack turns from yellow to brown by lunchtime.

- Your straw always floats up out of your soda can.

- The rings in your notebook are hard to open and close.

- Your badminton birdie always lands over the fence in the neighbor's yard.

- Your trampoline smells like sweaty socks.

# FIND OUT MORE

## Further Reading:

*Tinkering: Kids Learn by Making Stuff* by Curt Gabrielson

*Make: Paper Inventions: Machines That Move, Drawings That Light Up, and Wearables and Structures You Can Cut, Fold, and Roll* by Kathy Ceceri

*Make: Musical Inventions: DIY Instruments to Toot, Tap, Crank, Strum, Pluck, and Switch On* by Kathy Ceceri

*Engineering: Cool Women Who Design* by Vicki V. May

*National Geographic Kids Everything Robotics: All the Photos, Facts, and Fun to Make You Race for Robots* by Jennifer Swanson

*Try This!: 50 Fun Experiments for the Mad Scientist in You* by Karen Romano Young

*Flying Cars: The True Story* by Andrew Glass

## Websites to Visit:

Crash Course Kids, Engineering Playlist (YouTube), *youtube.com/user/crashcoursekids/playlists*

Design Squad, *pbskids.org/designsquad*

eGFI—Engineering Go For It, *egfi-k12.org*

Engineer Girl, *engineergirl.org*

Engineering for Kids With STEM, *engineeringforkids.com*

Sally Ride Science, *sallyridescience.com/stem-central*

Try Engineering through engineering- and technology-based games, *tryengineering.org/play-games*

USA Science and Engineering Festival, *usasciencefestival.org*

# GLOSSARY

## A

**ACOUSTIC:**
relating to sound or hearing

**AEROSPACE:**
the area that includes Earth's atmosphere and beyond

**AQUEDUCT:**
a bridge-like structure used to transport water

**AUTOMATE:**
to use machines, computers, or other systems to do work, instead of people

**AXLE:**
the bar on which a wheel turns; a simple machine when paired with a wheel

## B

**BRAINSTORM:**
to try to solve a problem by thinking of ideas

**BRONZE AGE:**
the period beginning between 3000 and 4000 B.C., when people used bronze to make tools and weapons, before iron was discovered around 1100 B.C.

**BULKHEAD:**
a wall that separates different parts of a ship

# C

**CATAPULT:**
an ancient weapon used to throw large objects, such as rocks

**COMPRESS:**
to press or squeeze something so that it becomes smaller or fits into a smaller space

**COMPRESSION WAVE:**
a vibration in the air, also called a sound or longitudinal wave

**CONSTRAINT:**
something that limits or prevents an action from working

**COUNTERWEIGHT:**
a weight that balances another weight

**CRITERION:**
(plural: criteria) a standard used to make a judgment

# E

**ENERGY:**
power that comes from heat, electricity, or other resources to perform work

**ENGINEER:**
a person trained to use math and science to design and build machines, products, systems, or structures

**ENGINEERING:**
the work of designing and building machines, products, systems, or structures

# F

**FLYING BUTTRESS:**
an arch that supports a building or wall from the outside

**FREESTANDING:**
not attached to or supported by anything else

**FREQUENCY:**
the number of times that something, such as a sound wave, is repeated within a time period

# G

**GRAVITY:**
the natural force that causes objects to fall toward Earth

**INTERNATIONAL SPACE STATION:**
the large spacecraft that orbits the Earth and serves as a science laboratory and home to astronauts and cosmonauts

# H

**HYDRAULICS:**
the science of using moving liquids to do work

# L

**LASER:**
a device that generates an intense, narrow beam of light

# I

**INCLINED PLANE:**
a simple machine consisting of a flat, sloping surface that is higher on one end; also called a ramp

**LEVER:**
a simple machine consisting of a bar or rod used to lift or move an object

**M**

**METAMATERIALS:**
engineered materials with qualities not usually found in nature

**N**

**NANOTECHNOLOGY:**
the science of working with atoms and molecules to build very small devices

**P**

**PROCESSING:**
a series of actions taken to treat or prepare something

**PROSTHETIC:**
a device used as a substitute for a missing or nonworking body part

**PROTOTYPE:**
the first version of something, used as a model to make improvements

**PULLEY:**
a simple machine consisting of a wheel with a grooved rim that holds a rope, used to change the direction of a force

**R**

**RATIONALE:**
a reason for doing or believing something

**RESEARCH:**
the act of collecting information on a subject

**S**

**SCREW:**
a simple machine consisting of an inclined plane made of a cylinder with spiral grooves that moves in circles to allow movement up and down or connect two objects together

**STRATEGY:**
a detailed plan to achieve a goal

**STRESS TEST:**
a process to determine if unfavorable conditions will damage a material, product, or structure

# T

**TECHNOLOGY:**
an object, system, or process created through science and engineering

**THERMAL:**
relating to heat

**THREE-DIMENSIONAL:**
having or appearing to have length, width, and depth

**TREBUCHET:**
a type of catapult that uses a counter-weight to hurl large stones or other missiles

**TRIAL AND ERROR:**
repeatedly testing an idea or process to find the best way to reach a solution

# W

**WEDGE:**
a simple machine that can be used to break objects apart or keep them together

# INDEX

Boldface indicates illustrations.

# PHOTO CREDITS

**COVER:** (bike tire with spokes), Ilya Andriyanov/iStockphoto/Getty Images; (colored pencils), Lukas Gojda/Shutterstock; (bolts), 123object/Shutterstock; (water faucet), Sergej Razvodovskij/Shutterstock; (red apple), yvdavyd/iStockphoto; (duct tape), Steve Collender/Shutterstock; (ball of twine), Olga Kovalenko/Shutterstock; (piece of twine), vesna cvorovic/Shutterstock; (cardboard rocket), ian nolan/Alamy Stock Photo; (paperclip), Jay Venkat/Shutterstock; (rubber ducky), Sergiy Kubyk/Shutterstock; (rope), Picsfive/Shutterstock; (striped straw), GooDween123/Shutterstock; (orange balloon), Bo Valentino/Shutterstock; (water bottle), Cloud7Days/Shutterstock; (bandages), Kitch Bain/Shutterstock; **SPINE:** (rubber ducky), Sergiy Kubyk/Shutterstock; **BACK COVER:** (rubber ducky), Sergiy Kubyk/Shutterstock; (robot hand), saginbay/Shutterstock; (black marker), Trinacria Photo/Shutterstock; (gears), GLYPHstock/Shutterstock

**INTERIOR:** (vector arrows throughout), johavel/Shutterstock; (duct tape pieces throughout), Steve Collender/Shutterstock; (paper with yellow paperclip throughout), vesna cvorovic/Shutterstock; (paper with tape throughout), vesna cvorovic/Shutterstock; (strip of tape throughout), Madlen/Shutterstock; (grid lined paper throughout), Thinkstock; (tiny grid lined paper throughout), Michael Travers/Shutterstock; (sketchy arrows throughout), pio3/Shutterstock; 1, Sergiy Kubyk/Shutterstock; 2, ian nolan/Alamy Stock Photo; 3 (ball of twine), Olga Kovalenko/Shutterstock; 3 (piece of twine), Hayati Kayhan/Shutterstock; 3 (paperclip), Jay Venkat/Shutterstock; 4 (UP), Morgan Lane Photography/Shutterstock; (LO), saginbay/Shutterstock; 5, (LE), Steven Bostock/Shutterstock; (UP RT), SeM/UIG via/Getty Images; (LO RT), Shevs/Shutterstock; 6-7, Jim Paillot

**SECTION 1: ALL ABOUT ENGINEERING:** 12 (UP), GLYPHstock/Shutterstock; 12 (CTR), irin-k/Shutterstock; 12 (LO), Ilya Andriyanov/iStockphoto/Getty Images; 13 (UP), lexaarts/Shutterstock; 13 (LO), saginbay/Shutterstock; 14 (UP), Digital Genetics/Shutterstock; 14 (CTR LE), Rawpixel/Shutterstock; 14 (CTR RT), U.S. Navy, Official Photograph; 14 (LO), photowind/Shutterstock; 15 (UP), Scanrail/Dreamstime; 15 (CTR LE), NASA; 15 (CTR RT), Anna Kucherova/Shutterstock; 15 (LO LE), Geo-grafika/iStockphoto; 15 (LO RT), ded pixto/Shutterstock; 16-17, Jim Paillot; 18 (UP), graja/Shutterstock; 18 (LO A, B, C), Mark Thiessen/NG Staff; 18 (LO D), Nikolais/Dreamstime; 18 (LO E), Feng Yu/Dreamstime; 18 (LO F), Sergej Razvodovskij/Shutterstock; 19 (pencil & shavings), spacezerocom/Shutterstock; 19 (all others), Mark Thiessen/NG Staff; 20 (UP), Morgan Lane Photography/Shutterstock; 20 (all others), Mark Thiessen/NG Staff; 21 (pencil & shavings), spacezerocom/Shutterstock; 23 (all others), Mark Thiessen/NG Staff; 22 (UP), PixieMe/Shutterstock; 22 (LE), FabrikaSimf/Shutterstock; 22 (LO), Shevs/Shutterstock; 22 (all others), Mark Thiessen/NG Staff; 23 (pencil & shavings), spacezerocom/Shutterstock; 23 (all others), Mark Thiessen/NG Staff; 24 (UP), Marina Lohrbach/Shutterstock; 24 (LO), kostudio/Shutterstock; 25 (UP), sakkmesterke/Shutterstock; 25 (CTR), PhotoBalance/Shutterstock; 25 (LO), Trinacria Photo/Shutterstock; 26, Sappington Todd/BloomImage RF/Getty Images; 26 (cat and books), Sanjida Rashid/NG Staff; 27 (LO LE), pixdeluxe/iStockphoto; 27 (UP RT), Photodisc; 27 (CTR RT), prapass/Shutterstock; 27 (LO A), Anton Starikov/Dreamstime; 27 (LO RT), Patchamol Jensatienwong/Shutterstock; 28 (UP LE), Gpointstudio/Dreamstime; 28 (LO LE), Shawn Hempel/Shutterstock; 28 (LO CTR), Eric Isselee/Shutterstock; 28 (LO RT), Tischenko Irina/Shutterstock; 29, Chones/Shutterstock; 30, LZ Image/Shutterstock; 31 (LO RT), Elnur/Shutterstock; 31 (sketches), Sanjida Rashid/NG Staff; 32 (UP), Sylwia Brataniec/Shutterstock; 32-33, Mark Thiessen/NG Staff; 34, aopsan/Shutterstock

**SECTION 2: SOLVE THIS!:** 38 (UP), Anna Hoychuk/Shutterstock; 38 (CTR), PhotoBalance/Shutterstock; 38 (LO), Africa Studio/Shutterstock; 39 (Constance), Randall Scott; 39 (Munazza), Munazza Alam; 39 (Ryan), Ryan Eagleson; 39 (UP LE), Olga Kovalenko/Shutterstock; 39 (UP RT), Hayati Kayhan/Shutterstock; 40 (Denise), Denise Pozzi-Escot; 40 (Cindy), Marie Freeman; 40 (Erika), Malvina Martin; 40 (Jeff), Jeffrey Marlow; 40 (Cecilia), Cecilia Mauricio; 41 (Eric), Lori Epstein; 41 (Tom), Tom O'Brien; 41 (Mike), Eric Berkenpass; 41 (Brad), Brad Henning; 41 (Joan), Rob Hislop;

**For Grant, who is adept at using the engineering approach to tackle problems, and for everyone who wonders what could be —JMG**

Since 1888, the National Geographic Society has funded more than 12,000 research, exploration, and preservation projects around the world. The Society receives funds from National Geographic Partners, LLC, funded in part by your purchase. A portion of the proceeds from this book supports this vital work. To learn more, visit natgeo.com/info.

For more information, visit nationalgeographic.com, call 1-800-647-5463, or write to the following address:

National Geographic Partners
1145 17th Street N.W.
Washington, D.C. 20036-4688 U.S.A.

Visit us online at nationalgeographic.com/books

For librarians and teachers: ngchildrensbooks.org

More for kids from National Geographic: kids.nationalgeographic.com

For information about special discounts for bulk purchases, please contact National Geographic Books Special Sales: specialsales@natgeo.com

For rights or permissions inquiries, please contact National Geographic Books Subsidiary Rights: bookrights@natgeo.com

Designed by Amanda Larsen and Sanjida Rashid

Trade paperback ISBN: 978-1-4263-2732-2
Reinforced library binding ISBN: 978-1-4263-2733-9

Printed in China
17/PPS/1

The author and publisher wish to thank the National Geographic explorers and engineers, who brought bundles of creativity; Jim Paillot and Sanjida Rashid for their lively and inspiring illustrations; and the dynamic, talented book team: Shelby Alinsky, Kathryn Williams, Amanda Larsen, Sanjida Rashid, Lori Epstein, Alix Inchausti, Anne LeongSon, and Gus Tello.